Lectionary Worship Aids: "Echoes Of The Word"

Series X, Cycle A

Ralph J. Mineo

CSS Publishing Company, Inc.
Lima, Ohio

LECTIONARY WORSHIP AIDS, SERIES X, CYCLE A

FIRST EDITION
Copyright © 2022
by CSS Publishing Co., Inc.

The original purchaser may print and photocopy material in this publication for use as it was intended (worship material for worship use; educational material for classroom use; dramatic material for staging or production). No additional permission is required from the publisher for such copying by the original purchaser only. Inquiries should be addressed to: Permissions, CSS Publishing Company, Inc., 5450 N. Dixie Highway, Lima, Ohio 45807.

Library of Congress Cataloging-in-Publication Data

Names: Mineo, Ralph J., 1950- author.
Title: Lectionary worship aids : echoes of the Word. Series X / Ralph J. Mineo.
Description: Lima : CSS Publishing Company, Inc., 2022- | Contents: [1] Cycle A
Identifiers: LCCN 2022028558 (print) | LCCN 2022028559 (ebook) | ISBN 9780788030505 (paperback) | ISBN 9780788030512 (adobe pdf)
Subjects: LCSH: Worship programs. | Common lectionary (1992)
Classification: LCC BV198 .M56 2022 (print) | LCC BV198 (ebook) | DDC 264--dc23/eng/20220805
LC record available at https://lccn.loc.gov/2022028558
LC ebook record available at https://lccn.loc.gov/2022028559

For more information about CSS Publishing Company resources, visit our website at www.csspub.com, email us at csr@csspub.com, or call (800) 241-4056.

e-book:
ISBN-13: 978-0-7880-3090-1
ISBN-10: 0-7880-3090-6

ISBN-13: 978-0-7880-3091-4
ISBN-10: 0-7880-3091-4

Table of Contents

Introduction And Suggestions 9

First Sunday of Advent 13

Second Sunday of Advent 17

Third Sunday of Advent 21

Fourth Sunday of Advent 25

Nativity of the Lord (Christmas) 29

First Sunday after Christmas Day 33

Second Sunday after Christmas Day 36

Epiphany of the Lord 40

Baptism of the Lord / First Sunday after the Epiphany / Ordinary Time 1 44

Second Sunday after the Epiphany / Ordinary Time 2 48

Third Sunday after the Epiphany /
Ordinary Time 3 52

Fourth Sunday after the Epiphany /
Ordinary Time 4 56

Fifth Sunday after the Epiphany /
Ordinary Time 5 60

Sixth Sunday after the Epiphany /
Proper 1 / Ordinary Time 6 64

Seventh Sunday after the Epiphany / Proper 2 / Ordinary Time 7 68

Transfiguration Sunday / Last Sunday after the Epiphany 72

Ash Wednesday 76

First Sunday in Lent 80

Second Sunday in Lent	84
Third Sunday in Lent	88
Fourth Sunday in Lent	92
Fifth Sunday in Lent	96
Palm Sunday / Sunday of the Passion	100
Maundy Thursday	104
Good Friday	108
Resurrection of the Lord / Easter Sunday	112
Second Sunday of Easter	116
Third Sunday of Easter	120
Fourth Sunday of Easter	124
Fifth Sunday of Easter	128
Sixth Sunday of Easter	132
Ascension of the Lord	136
Seventh Sunday of Easter	140
Day of Pentecost	144
Trinity Sunday	148
Proper 3 / Ordinary Time 8	152
Proper 4 / Ordinary Time 9	156
Proper 5 / Ordinary Time 10	160
Proper 6 / Ordinary Time 11	164
Proper 7 / Ordinary Time 12	168

Proper 8 / Ordinary Time 13 172
Proper 9 / Ordinary Time 14 176
Proper 10 / Ordinary Time 15 180
Proper 11 / Ordinary Time 16 184
Proper 12 / Ordinary Time 17 188
Proper 13 / Ordinary Time 18 192
Proper 14 / Ordinary Time 19 196
Proper 15 / Ordinary Time 20 200
Proper 16 / Ordinary Time 21 204
Proper 17 / Ordinary Time 22 208
Proper 18 / Ordinary Time 23 212
Proper 19 / Ordinary Time 24 216
Proper 20 / Ordinary Time 25 220
Proper 21 / Ordinary Time 26 224
Proper 22 / Ordinary Time 27 228
Proper 23 / Ordinary Time 28 232
Proper 24 / Ordinary Time 29 236
Proper 25 / Ordinary Time 30 240
Proper 26 / Ordinary Time 31 244
Proper 27 / Ordinary Time 32 248
Proper 28 / Ordinary Time 33 252
Reign of Christ / Christ the King 256
Reformation 260

All Saints 264

Thanksgiving 268

APPENDIX 1 273

APPENDIX 2 275

*Dedicated to
Jo Mineo,
my partner
in life
and
in ministry.*

*"Thank you, Lord, that she loves me."
Words I wrote in her signature song "Butterflies and Penguins."*

Introduction And Suggestions

I love liturgy! As a pastor in a mainline church, it's not unusual to hear criticisms of structured liturgy. After several years of experience, I stopped being defensive. Instead, I made a request: "Do me a favor. Ask some young people in my congregation, including teenagers, what they think about liturgy." No one has ever followed up with me on that request, but I'm certain they would have heard positive responses from many of the young people. Liturgy has a spiritual appeal. It resonates in the soul. As people are learning the ways of spirituality, the repetition in liturgy creates holy rhythm, holy cadence. Liturgy can be educational and very often elicits inadvertent memorization. I love liturgy!

The word liturgy, from the Greek, literally means "work of the people." This volume of liturgical pieces includes responses and prayers that directly involve the people. Most are in dialogic form. The theme of each worship service is based on assigned lectionary texts of the day. For dialogues in this volume, the regular font is for the worship leader(s). The **bold text** is for members of the assembly. Some users may prefer to designate "Leader" or "Pastor" and "People" or "All" in front of those sections.

This volume includes all the Sundays assigned in Cycle "A" with some special services added. Not all Sundays appear in a given calendar year. Therefore, there are several extra liturgical pieces that could be used as substitutes or in other settings.

I've subtitled this volume "Echoes Of The Word" because the intent is to hear parts of the assigned lectionary readings in a sentence, a phrase, sometimes a single word. The echoes can serve as anticipation, when used before the readings, or as reinforcement, after the readings have been heard. The repetition and echoes in this volume, it's my hope, is to help you create holy rhythms for worship.

Call to Worship

For this ritual, references to one or more of the texts is generally very evident. My hope is that, right from the beginning of worship, the importance of the scripture readings of the day is lifted up.

Collect / Prayer of the Day

This prayer is directly based on one or more of the readings. Since some liturgists might prefer to use the assigned prayers in their lectionary, this could be used or adapted elsewhere in the service, for example as a sermon prelude or postlude prayer, even as an offertory prayer. I've formatted the prayer as a unison prayer of the assembly, but it could easily be adapted for the presider to lead with the people responding "Amen."

Confession / Assurance of Forgiveness

The "Rite Of Confession" is generally placed at the beginning of worship. I often like to include this rite after the readings and the sermon, as a response to hearing the word. The "echoes" are very clear when included at this point in the service.

Prayers of the People / Prayers of Intercession

In a familiar format, there is a dialogue added at the end of each paragraph of the prayers. These prayers may be knit into a single pastoral prayer by omitting these responses. I recommend adding at least one prayer based something happening in the world, or something relating to your specific community of faith. I've included some prayers for special occasions in Appendix 1.

Sending Dialogue

The "Sending Dialogue" parallels the style of the "Call to Worship." The basic purpose of this dialogue is to lift up some ways to put God's word into practice in daily living. A blessing or benediction would immediately follow this dialogue. If you choose not to include this liturgical section, you could easily translate it into a benediction. For example, change "We will walk with God daily..." to simply "Walk with God daily..."

Hymns

I've included ten hymns for each worship service. This was unexpectedly a very enlightening and devotional part of writing this volume, mostly because I learned several new hymns. I would suggest that, if you see an unfamiliar title, check it out. You may not use the hymn in your worship service, but, as an echo of God's word, it could help in your preparation. There are over 400 hymn titles included in this volume.

Alternative Uses For This Volume

Some who receive this volume will not use all the liturgical pieces for worship. Here are some alternative ideas for using this book:

Help For Sermon Preparation. Beginning at least one week before your sermon, (1) read all the scripture passages of the day, (2) pray through these liturgical dialogues and prayers for your personal devotions, (3) highlight or jot down words, phrases, or ideas that come to you.

Devotional Book. Not exclusively for pastors and worship leaders, this volume could be a personal prayer book for anyone. It could be used the week before, or the week after, a given worship service. Even if you don't follow the lectionary for worship, there is certainly value in reading these texts and praying these prayers as part of your devotional life.

Bible Study. If you have a sermon preparation group, a Bible Study, or a Sunday school class based on lectionary, parts of the liturgy could be used for opening or closing prayer.

In Conclusion

This is going to happen: you will dislike a particular wording, approach, even a theological misstep on my part. Again, I say, it's going to happen. (I assure you, after this material is published, I'll find such things myself!) In that light, I would like to suggest that you not dwell on such missteps. Instead, edit, adapt, and translate them for your use. My hope is that the volume will be a stepping stone or a springboard for your work, your liturgy, your preparations for the "work of the people."

Writing this volume was both a creative and devotional experience for me. I always began by praying for the inspiration of the Holy Spirit,* and then let the words of the text echo in my mind, heart, and soul.

Now, it's your turn. You are welcome to use these pieces exactly as included herein. Alternatively, I invite and encourage you to invoke your own creativity, revising according to your inclinations and the movement of the Holy Spirit within you.

Finally, let the word of God echo in your mind, heart, and soul!

Blessings on your reading of God's word!

Blessings on all your worship preparations!

Blessings on your ministry!

*Disclaimer: All mistakes are mine, not the Holy Spirit's!

First Sunday of Advent

Isaiah 2:1-5
Psalm 122
Romans 13:11-14
Matthew 24:36-44

Call to Worship
These are the days of hopeful watching and waiting.
We go up to the house of God.

Give thanks to the holy name of God.
All thanks and praise to God, our God.

We gather here as children of God.
We will seek goodness and peace for all children of God.

Collect / Prayer of the Day
God of our salvation, awaken our hearts and make us ready for your presence in our lives. Prepare us to receive you with joy and gladness. Help us to lay aside works of darkness. Guide us in the ways of peace. Teach us to walk honorably in your light, in the name of Jesus. Amen.

Confession / Assurance of Forgiveness
These are the days of hopeful watching and waiting.
Salvation is near to us. The time to be awake is now.

We confess our sins and commit ourselves to lay aside the works of darkness.
{silent prayer for personal confession of sins}

God, our God, we confess that we have walked in darkness. We have sinned against others in ways that have harmed them, and ourselves. We have centered our lives on our own needs at the expense of others, and at the expense of goodness, kindness, and truth. Shine the light of your forgiveness upon us, that we might live honorably. Clothe us with the armor of your light, that we might walk in your ways, now and always. Amen.

God's light is shining upon you. God's love is embracing you. God's presence is forgiving you. Therefore, rejoice in ✠ Jesus Christ our Lord.
Amen.

Prayers of the People / Prayers of Intercession

God, our God, who made the stars and the planets, who gives life to all living things, we give you thanks for the beauty around us, and for our very lives. God of hope,
Hear our prayer.

We give thanks to your holy name. We pray in gratitude for your daily care for us, for your grace and favor, for your goodness that is present in the world. We give you thanks for the hope of eternal joy. God of hope,
Hear our prayer.

We pray that you guide the leaders of every nation into the pathways of peace, that swords be turned into plowshares, that weapons be turned into food and nourishment for the hungry. Renew the world that we might live in peace. God of hope,
Hear our prayer.

We pray for troubled families and relationships, especially those in deep distress and those who struggle with brokenness, quarreling, jealousy, and sins of every kind. We pray that all your children lay aside works of darkness, that your Son, our Lord

Jesus Christ will come down and clothe us all with your armor of divine light. God of hope,
Hear our prayer.

We pray that your presence in the world would soften hardened hearts and inspire all people to care for each other with kindness, gentleness, and holy love. God of hope,
Hear our prayer.

We pray for your healing grace that the sick among us will be sustained and strengthened. *(Specific names are included here).* God of hope,
Hear our prayer.

As we await the day when there will be no more suffering and sorrow, bestow comfort and hope upon the broken-hearted. Remembering loved ones, we pray that your Holy Spirit embrace all who grieve. God of hope,
Hear our prayer.

Hear our prayers, O God, and send us, and the whole world, your Holy Spirit, that we all grow into the likeness of Jesus Christ, our Lord and Savior.
Amen.

Sending Dialogue

These are the days of hopeful watching and waiting.
We ready ourselves for the coming of the Lord.

Make way for peace in the world.
For the sake of our relatives and friends, we will proclaim peace.

For the sake of all the children of God, may God's peace be known.
We will bring peace and hope to the world.

Hymns

Arise, Your Light Has Come
Christ, Be Our Light!
Hark! A Thrilling Voice Is Sounding
Jesus Came, The Heavens Adoring
The King Shall Come When Morning Dawns
Lo! He Comes With Clouds Descending
My Lord, What A Morning
Oh, Come, Oh, Come, Emmanuel
Rejoice, Rejoice, Believers
Savior Of The Nations, Come

Second Sunday of Advent

Isaiah 11:1-10
Psalm 72:1-7, 18-19
Romans 15:4-13
Matthew 3:1-12

Call to Worship
These are the days of watching and waiting for peace.
Blessed be the God of our salvation.

God is our defender and judge.
Blessed be the God of justice and peace.

God is our protector and deliverer.
Blessed be the God of righteousness who does wondrous things.

Collect / Prayer of the Day
Steadfast God, protect and defend us from every evil, and guide us away from unrighteousness. Nourish us that we always produce good fruit in your kingdom, fruit of righteousness and justice, fruit of hope, joy, and peace. Encourage us through your word to live in harmony with one another and glorify you with one voice, through Jesus Christ our Lord. Amen.

Confession / Assurance of Forgiveness
These are the days of watching and waiting for peace.
The kingdom of God has come near.

We prepare the way of the Lord by confessing our sins.
{silent prayer for personal confession of sins}

We confess, O God, that we have wandered from your pathways, not obeying your commandments. Come Holy Spirit, rest upon us now. Give us wisdom and understanding. Judge us according to divine righteousness and grace. Forgive us and wash away all evil and sinfulness, that our hearts may be a glorious dwelling place of divine goodness, in the name of Christ Jesus, our Lord. Amen.

Rejoice in the name of Jesus Christ, the one who came down and lived among us, who welcomed us into the glory of God. Rejoice in the forgiveness of your sins, and bear fruit worthy of repentance, in the name of ✠ Jesus Christ our Lord.
Amen.

Prayers of the People / Prayers of Intercession

Creator God, who made the world beautiful and majestic, we give you thanks for the gift of life and for the wonders of all creation. God of peace,
Hear our prayer.

We thank you for all the people and relationships that enrich our lives, for those who encourage and protect us, for those who guide and teach us, for those who challenge us and call out the best in us. God of peace,
Hear our prayer.

We ask you to bless and give healing grace to every difficult, stressful, and hurting relationship. We pray that those who are struggling will find peace. We pray for the protection and healing of victims of abuse and terror, and those who are treated with contempt and hatefulness. God of peace,
Hear our prayer.

Shine your light into the darkness of the world. Guide leaders of the nations into the paths of righteousness, bearing fruits of

repentance, justice, goodness, and peace. God of peace,
Hear our prayer.

Come to us with new and exciting insights. Surprise us with your grace. Equip us with deeper faith. Encourage us to live in harmony with one another. Strengthen us with the hope of your Holy Spirit. God of peace,
Hear our prayer.

We pray for those in need of deliverance from physical sickness and ailments of the heart. *(Specific names are included here)*. God of peace,
Hear our prayer.

As we remember the lives of our loved ones who have died, comfort us and fill our hearts with the assurance of your eternal kingdom. God of peace,
Hear our prayer.

We pray to you, O God, that your holy and divine peace and presence flow freely into our hearts, into this household of faith, into all the nations, and into all your creation, through Christ Jesus, our Lord.
Amen.

Sending Dialogue

These are the days of watching and waiting for peace.
Blessed be God's glorious name forever!

By the way you live, bear fruit worthy of repentance and love.
We will prepare the way of the Lord!

May the God of hope fill you and all creation with joy and peace.
May God's glory fill the whole earth!

Hymns
All Hail The Power Of Jesus' Name
Awake! Awake, And Greet The New Morn
Come, Thou Long Expected Jesus
Jesus Shall Reign
On Jordan's Banks The Baptist's Cry
People, Look East
Prepare The Royal Highway
Soul, Adorn Yourself With Gladness
There's A Voice In The Wilderness Crying
Wild And Lone The Prophet's Voice

Third Sunday of Advent

Isaiah 35:1-10
Psalm 146:5-10 or Luke 1:46b-55
James 5:7-10
Matthew 11:2-11

Call to Worship
These are the days of joyful watching and waiting.
Our hope is in God, the creator, who made heaven and earth, the sea, and all that is in them.

We sing for joy to the God of our salvation.
We rejoice in God, who opens our eyes and sets us free.

With all generations, we rejoice in God.
Everlasting joy and gladness shall be upon us.

Collect / Prayer of the Day
God, our God, strengthen our hearts as we prepare for your nearness. Open the doors of your kingdom and draw us near to you. Make our way holy and come to save us. Send us as messengers to bring your joy, peace, and love into the wilderness of this generation, that none may go astray. We pray in the name of Jesus, who comes among us with the good news of the kingdom of heaven. Amen.

Confession / Assurance of Forgiveness
These are the days of joyful watching and waiting.
And yet, the sin around us and within us brings sadness and despair.

As a faith community, we return to the Lord by confessing our sins.
{silent prayer for personal confession of sins}

Holy God, you surround us with grace. You embrace us with love. You gather us into a family of faith. Yet we continue to linger in the realms of sin. We persist in the ways that disconnect us from one another. Our words and actions cause harm. Forgive us our sins and let the harmful ways of selfishness and sin depart from our lives. Stir our hearts and souls to return to you and obtain your grace and love, your joy and gladness. We pray in Jesus' name. Amen.

Truly I tell you, the Lord God sets you free from the prisons of sin. The glory of God's majesty is before you. Here is your God, who makes you clean, and leads you in the paths of holiness. Forgiveness and everlasting joy are upon you, through the life, death, and resurrection of ✠ Jesus Christ our Lord.
Amen.

Prayers of the People / Prayers of Intercession

God, our salvation, we pray for the peace of the nations of the world. Instill in every ruler and leader a desire for peace. We pray that people would learn to respect others, that exploitation and evil would come to an end. We pray that all the nations strive to live together with mercy, peace, and harmony. God of joy,
Hear our prayer.

We pray that the church in the world be a living witness, showing forth your love and mercy, your divine justice and peace. God of joy,
Hear our prayer.

We pray that you strengthen our hearts with patience, tolerance, and love for one another. Teach us to put an end to grumbling and harshness toward others. God of joy,
Hear our prayer.

Send your good news to all who suffer physically, emotionally, and spiritually. Send ministers of good news to the poor, the blind, the deaf, and all with disabilities. Open everyone's hearts and minds to be blessed and challenged by Jesus, your Son. God of joy,
Hear our prayer.

As we watch and wait for the Savior, grant us the joy of your salvation. Free us from bondage to sinfulness. Grant us generous and patient hearts that bloom in the harshest seasons of our lives. God of joy,
Hear our prayer.

We pray for the sick and suffering, that your presence will bring healing and hope. *(Specific names are included here).* God of joy,
Hear our prayer.

We pray for those coping with death. Where there is grief, where tears abound, and where pain overwhelms, send hope and peace to your children. God of joy,
Hear our prayer.

As our prayer ascends to you, O God of joy, we are confident that you hear us. Restore us to the joy of your salvation, in the name of Jesus Christ, our Lord.
Amen.

Sending Dialogue

These are the days of joyful watching and waiting.
We will carry good news to a world with an overwhelming need for God's mercy.

As you go forth, you will encounter people in the world who are weak and filled with fear.
We will carry the strength of God's love and mercy with us wherever we go.

You will encounter sadness, grief, and pain in the days ahead.
We will carry with us the promise of the everlasting joy of God's kingdom.

Hymns

Christ Is Made The Sure Foundation
Come, Thou Long-Expected Jesus
Joy To The World
My Jesus, I Love Thee
O For A Thousand Tongues
O Jesus, Joy of Loving Hearts
Open My Eyes, That I May See
Rejoice, Rejoice, Believers
Savior Of The Nations, Come
The Advent Of Our God

Fourth Sunday of Advent

Isaiah 7:10-16
Psalm 80:1-7, 17-19
Romans 1:1-7
Matthew 1:18-25

Call to Worship
These are the days of watching and waiting for love.
The face of our Lord God shines upon us.

God will restore and save us.
Stir up your love, O God. Come to save us!

Listen, you people of God, and you will receive a sign.
A son will be born among us, and he will be named Jesus.

Collect / Prayer of the Day
O God of salvation, by the Holy Spirit, your Son, Jesus our Lord, is always with us. Give us grace, and strengthen our faith, that we would become more obedient to your will as we celebrate your love among us. Hear our prayers, take away our fears, and give us your life and love, in the name of the one who is named Jesus. Amen.

Confession / Assurance of Forgiveness
These are the days of watching and waiting for love.
These are the days of open hearts.

We now openly and honestly confess our sins to our God of love.
{silent prayer for personal confession of sins}

Eternal God of love, we confess that our hearts are sometimes unprepared for your coming. We have turned from your will and your ways. We have ignored your presence and your grace. We have been rebellious and disobedient. For the sake of Jesus Christ, to whom we belong, open our minds and hearts to your presence, that we may receive your words and your Spirit of love. Make our hearts ready to welcome him in whose name we pray, Jesus our Lord. Amen.

As ones invited to do God's will, hear this good news: God our Father comes to you now with grace and peace, and forgives your sins, through ✠ Jesus Christ, our Lord and Savior.
Amen.

Prayers of the People / Prayers of Intercession

Hear our prayers, loving God, that the church will now and always be a sign of your presence, especially in the darkness, trials, and struggles of daily living. God of love,
Hear our prayer.

We pray that the world would put away weapons of war and embrace the ways of peace. God of love,
Hear our prayer.

Inspire all world leaders to work together to bring about peace and justice for all people. God of love,
Hear our prayer.

We pray for your Holy Spirit to touch and inspire all who are seeking meaning, vocations, and purpose in life. Send them your divine love and care. God of love,
Hear our prayer.

We pray that the homeless find shelter, that the hungry be fed, that those in harm's way be protected, that those who need jobs

find work, that those living with despair find hope, that the lonely and the lost receive love.
Hear our prayer.

We pray for all who suffer with physical or mental illness. Make them strong through the healing presence of Jesus. *(Specific names are included here)*. God of love,
Hear our prayer.

We pray for those who mourn, as they ponder memories of those they have loved. Comfort them with the joy of resurrection and assurance of eternal life. God of love,
Hear our prayer.

God-with-us, send signs of your love into the world, and by your Holy Spirit open our minds to recognize those signs as holy and blessed. Draw us, and all people, to become more and more aware of your presence in our lives, through Christ our Lord.
Amen.

Sending Dialogue

These are the days of watching and waiting for love.
We will live our daily lives seeing God's love around and within us.

As you live in a waiting, needy world, God anoints you to proclaim good news.
We will proclaim the good news of God's ever-present love.

The Spirit of God is upon you.
We will show God's love in our words and in our actions.

Hymns

All Hail To Thee, Immanuel!
Hail To The Lord's Anointed
Hark! The Herald Angels Sing
Joy To The World
Oh, Come, Oh, Come, Emmanuel
Rejoice, Rejoice, Believers
Savior Of The Nations, Come
Spirit Of Holiness, Descend
That Beautiful Name
The King Of Love My Shepherd Is

Nativity of the Lord (Christmas)

Isaiah 9:2-7
Psalm 96
Titus 2:11-14
Luke 2:1-14 [15-20]

Call to Worship

The grace of God has appeared.
Glory to God in the highest heaven! Peace on earth!

Worship the Lord in holy splendor.
Glory to God in the highest heaven! Peace on earth!

Let the heavens be glad and let the earth rejoice.
Glory to God in the highest heaven! Peace on earth!

Collect / Prayer of the Day

Mighty God, everlasting Father, we sing for joy as we celebrate the good news of the birth of Jesus, our Messiah, Lord, and Savior. We glorify and praise you by living godly lives. Just as we are eager to come into your presence, we are eager to share your love with the world. As we celebrate this good news of joy for all people, we glorify and praise you all our days, in the name of the one who came down to redeem us, Jesus Christ, our Savior. Amen.

Confession / Assurance of Forgiveness

Come, O Lord, and abide with us.
It is our desire that we abide in you.

With the holy gift of God's Son before us, we examine our hearts and confess our sins.
{silent prayer for personal confession of sins}

Holy God, giver of life, we confess and repent of every moment we have turned from your love and grace. We confess and repent of the times we have turned away from each other, being unkind, uncaring, unloving. We have spoken and acted against your holy will for us. We have not done the good to which we are called. As we stand together, remembering the birth of love into the world, forgive us and help us to forgive one another, in the holy name of Jesus. Amen.

The good news of the gospel is this: the love of God is abundant and is the power to overcome sin and disobedience. By the grace of the one born on that night in Bethlehem, God forgives your sins through ✠ Jesus Christ, our Lord.
Amen.

Prayers of the People / Prayers of Intercession

God of life, we thank you for the goodness and love of this holy season, for family gatherings, and for friendships that celebrate your presence among us. We pray:
Hear us, God of love.

We pray for every corner of the world which is in turmoil and does not have peace. Direct and guide all who govern that they would recognize your presence and make decisions which will bring peace to all the world. We pray:
Hear us, God of love.

In every Christmas celebration of our day, point your children to the one who is the center of our joy, Jesus our Lord. We pray:
Hear us, God of love.

In these days of celebration, we pray for those who are cold or lonely or forgotten. We pray for those who are unable to celebrate, those who are hungry, those who are depressed, those who are addicted, those who are troubled, those who are suffering. We pray:
Hear us, God of love.

We pray for those who have no place to rest their heads, refugees who struggle with the bitter trials of flight and exile. We pray for all who are lost. Send angels, stars, your church, to guide them to your love. We pray:
Hear us, God of love.

We pray for the sick, the hospitalized, all in need of healing. Along with caregivers, send your healing and grace into the lives of your children. *(Specific names are included here)*. We pray:
Hear us, God of love.

Let your light and glory be born in the hearts of all who are grieving in this season of love. Be present with them in their moments of distress, bless their tears and their memories, embrace them in their every emotion. We pray:
Hear us, God of love.

Good and gracious God, your Word has become flesh in our midst. Hear our prayers and help us to recognize your presence in our own hearts, in every person, and in the whole world. We pray in the name of the one who comes down to be born into our lives, Jesus Christ, our Savior.
Amen.

Sending Dialogue

O sing to the Lord! Sing a new song!
We sing to the Lord! We bless God's holy name!

Tell of God's salvation from day to day.
We will proclaim: a Savior is born, who is Christ the Lord!

Glorify and praise God for all you had heard and seen!
We will declare God's glory here and among all the peoples!

Hymns

Away In A Manger
Angels We Have Heard On High
Go Tell It On The Mountain
Hark! The Herald Angels Sing
Joy To The World
Love Has Come
O Little Town Of Bethlehem
Of The Father's Love Begotten
Oh, Come, All Ye Faithful
The First Noel

First Sunday after Christmas Day

Isaiah 63:7-9
Psalm 148
Hebrews 2:10-18
Matthew 2:13-23

Call to Worship
Praise the Lord from the heavens. Praise God all the earth.
Praise God forever and ever.

All creatures and all of nature, praise God.
Praise God forever and ever.

All you faithful people, praise God.
Praise God forever and ever.

Collect / Prayer of the Day
Heavenly Father, you have redeemed us. You have lifted us up and carried us. You have made us sisters and brothers of our Lord Jesus. In the midst of the congregation, we praise you and sanctify your holy name. Attentive to suffering, violence, and weeping, we plead with you to send your mercy and comfort into all the world, in the name of Christ Jesus, our Lord. Amen.

Confession / Assurance of Forgiveness
Let us live fully as children of God.
We will bear the light of Christ to all whom we meet.

We confess our sins, the darkness of our lives.
{silent prayer for personal confession of sins}

Holy One, we confess that we have traveled to dark places, turning away from your divine light. We confess that we have not allowed your good news to change our lives. We confess we have neglected service in your kingdom. Shine your light into our daily lives and awaken your grace within us. Enable us to unite our lives with your divine will, in the name of Jesus, our Savior. Amen.

Behold, God is your salvation. Trust in God and do not fear, for the Lord God is your strength and your song. God forgives your sins in ✠ Jesus Christ, who is your salvation.
Amen.

Prayers of the People / Prayers of Intercession

God of salvation, guide and lead the church and each local community to proclaim the good news and witness to your presence in the world. Lord of love,
Hear our prayer.

Help us, O God, to speak and act on behalf of every innocent one who suffers because of the darkness of sin, violence, evil words, and actions. Protect the innocent ones. Lord of love,
Hear our prayer.

Come to us again in our time, that the fire of your love would burn away the coldness of the hatred, greed, and selfishness that abounds in the world. Lord of love,
Hear our prayer.

We pray for the world, that nations would make pathways to peace. Raise up leaders who are open to following your will and your ways. Lord of love,
Hear our prayer.

We pray for those who are struggling with hardship or suffering. Help them to know of your love and care for them. Be born in us, and in the hearts of everyone in the world. Lord of love,
Hear our prayer.

We pray for healing for those who are sick, and for strength for those who are struggling and troubled. Protect all your children from harm. *(Specific names are included here)*. Lord of love,
Hear our prayer.

As we especially remember those who have died at the hands of evildoers, we also remember all those in our families and in this community of faith who have gone before us. We pray that all those who are grieving receive comfort and care. Lord of love,
Hear our prayer.

Gracious God, whose Word has become flesh, give ear to our every need. Help us to experience and welcome your presence in this holy season. We pray in the name of Jesus.
Amen.

Sending Dialogue

Let us live fully as children of God.
We will bear the light of Christ to all whom we meet.

Jesus came that we might have fullness of life.
We will strive to grow closer to God, day by day.

God calls us into divine partnership.
We will serve others in the name of Jesus.

Hymns

Good Christian Friends, Rejoice
Hark! The Herald Angels Sing
In The Bleak Midwinter
Infant Holy, Infant Lowly
It Came Upon The Midnight Clear
O Love, How Deep, How Broad, How High
Of the Father's Love Begotten
To Us A Child Of Hope Is Born
Unto Us A Boy Is Born
What Child Is This?

Second Sunday after Christmas Day

Jeremiah 31:7-14
Psalm 147:12-20
Ephesians 1:3-14
John 1:[1-9] 10-18

Call to Worship
Blessed be the God and Father of our Lord Jesus Christ.
God has blessed us in Christ with every spiritual blessing.

Through Jesus Christ, we are destined us to be God's children.
Blessed be the God and Father of our Lord Jesus Christ.

In Christ, we were marked with the seal of the Holy Spirit.
We are God's own people, and we praise God's glory.

Collect / Prayer of the Day
Blessed are you, O Lord our God. You choose us before the foundation of the world. You destined us, in divine love, to be your children. You marked us with the seal of your Holy Spirit. Open our hearts and minds this day, that we may hear your word clearly, and receive your gifts to the praise of your glory, in Christ Jesus, our Lord. Amen.

Confession / Assurance of Forgiveness
The light shines in the darkness, and the darkness did not overcome it.
The Word became flesh and lived among us.

We confess our sins and the darkness of our hearts.
{silent prayer for personal confession of sins}

God, our God, we have embraced darkness, even closing our eyes to your light. You came to give us life, and we chose the ways that lead to darkness, even death. We have chosen to separate ourselves from your will. We have gone astray. Now, we pray, open our eyes to see the light of your grace. Open our ears to hear your voice of love. Open our minds to understand and accept your divine forgiveness, your healing, your peace. In the name of Christ Jesus, we pray. Amen.

In the fullness of Christ, you have received grace upon grace. In him, you have heard the word of truth, the gospel of our salvation. Accept redemption as God's own children. For you are reconciled to the divine, grace-filled heart of God. Believe in God who forgives you, in ✠ Jesus Christ, our Savior and Lord.
Amen.

Prayers of the People / Prayers of Intercession

We thank you, loving God, for every joy of living, for the gift of amazing grace, for the joy of relationships, and for the divine love we receive every day. We pray to the Lord.
Lord, hear our prayer.

We thank you for those who labor for the well-being of your people. Strengthen and nourish them, and send your ministers to them with food, shelter, and love. We pray to the Lord.
Lord, hear our prayer.

We pray that you inspire the nations to choose a straight path. Make the people of world safe, that they would not stumble, and not become scattered. We pray that the leaders of every nation would follow your holy will. We pray to the Lord.
Lord, hear our prayer.

We pray for your blessings upon all the children of the world. Grant peace, fill everyone with the finest of wheat, with wisdom and insight, with every spiritual blessing in the heavenly places. We pray to the Lord.
Lord, hear our prayer.

We pray for those who live in the darkness of sin, despair, depression, addiction, anger – any darkness of the heart, mind, body, and soul. Send your light, your healing, your guidance, your grace. We pray to the Lord.
Lord, hear our prayer.

We pray for your healing graces to be with all who are sick. *(Specific names are included here)*. We pray to the Lord.
Lord, hear our prayer.

As we remember those living in your eternal light, having received their divine inheritance, bless the tears and anxieties of all the grieving ones traveling this earthly journey. Turn their mourning into joy. We pray to the Lord.
Lord, hear our prayer.

God of heaven, who made the light of Christ shine, shattering the darkness of the world, send that same light into our daily lives, and into the lives of all for whom we pray. In Jesus' name.
Amen.

Sending Dialogue
The true light which enlightens us all has come into the world.
We go with God's true light within us.

God have given us the power to live as God's own children.
We will live and walk as God's children.

Jesus, God's only Son, is close to the Father's heart.
We will also remain close to the Father's heart, all our days.

Hymns

Go Tell It On The Mountain
God Of Our Life, Through All The Circling Years
Lo, How A Rose Is Growing
Love Has Come
O God, Our Help In Ages Past
O Word Of God Incarnate
Of The Father's Love Begotten
Once In Royal David's City
The Word Of God Was From The Start
Thy Strong Word

Epiphany of the Lord

Isaiah 60:1-6
Psalm 72:1-7, 10-14
Ephesians 3:1-12
Matthew 2:1-12

Call to Worship
Arise, shine! Your light has come!
The glory of the Lord God has risen upon us.

Darkness covers the earth, and all people.
But the glory of God rises up and appears over us.

Lift up your eyes and look around.
We praise God as we journey together.

Collect / Prayer of the Day
Holy God, who created all things, your light has come, and we see your light in the face of Jesus Christ, our Lord. Through him, you guide our journey away from sin and evil, to receive your grace and love. Through him, you strengthen us to resist temptation, to do your work of service in the world. Through him, you move us away from darkness, to journey in your marvelous light toward our heavenly, eternal home. According to your eternal purpose, continue to guide, strengthen, and lead your church. With boldness and confidence, we pray in the name of Jesus Christ, our Lord. Amen.

Confession / Assurance of Forgiveness
We have observed the Son of God coming into our world.
His light has come, and his glory has risen upon us.

As the Magi traveled to Jesus, we now travel to him, in our hearts, for forgiveness.
{silent prayer for personal confession of sins}

God of light, we confess that we have wandered into darkness, even remaining there. We have been blind to human need and suffering. We have failed to forgive others as we have been forgiven. Accept our repentance, O Lord, and restore us. Let your light shine upon us. Forgive us and lead us out of the darkness of sin and wrongdoing. In Jesus' name. Amen.

Know this: God had sought to reconcile you in love and forgiveness before you ever thought about seeking God. Accept now the shining light of God's glory upon you. Let your heart rejoice in the power and in the grace of God. For God forgives your sins through ✠ Jesus Christ, our Lord.
Amen.

Prayers of the People / Prayers of Intercession

God of light, we pray today that your kingdom will extend to all corners of the world, that your grace become light for all people. We pray together,
Grant us your light, O Lord.

Grant blessings upon the leaders of all nations, that they would turn away from all evil and violence, that they would become instruments of peace, truth, and well-being, and that they would act according to your will. We pray together,
Grant us your light, O Lord.

Open the eyes and hearts of those blinded by pride, arrogance, and greed. Let all the people of the world see daily signs of your goodness and love, that everyone would walk in the light of your Son, in the pathways of your grace. We pray together,
Grant us your light, O Lord.

Send the light and radiance of your love to those who live their days in darkness. Give us courage to let your light shine through us. We pray together,
Grant us your light, O Lord.

As the magi traveled in great joy to worship your Son, guide us by your Holy Spirit to be witnesses to your grace-filled light. Inspire us to speak holy words, and to live holy and wholesome lives. We pray together,
Grant us your light, O Lord.

Watch over our loved ones. Encourage the afflicted. Give hope to those in despair. Comfort those who grieve. Grant healing to those who struggle with sickness. *(Specific names are included here)*. We pray together,
Grant us your light, O Lord.

As we remember those who have gone before us, as memories and signs of their love come to us, shine your light upon these memories and signs, upon the tears and the laughter. Help us to travel in your light, and, even in grief, help us to experience your presence in our lives. We pray together,
Grant us your light, O Lord.

We thank you, O God, for every sign of your loving presence in our lives and in the world. We bring you our requests, our prayers of thanksgiving, and our joyful praise, in the name of Jesus Christ our Lord.
Amen.

Sending Dialogue

Arise, shine, for your light has come!
We will proclaim praise to the Lord!

The eternal purpose that God has carried out in Christ Jesus our Lord has been revealed to you.
We will walk in faith with boldness and confidence.

The glory of the Lord has risen upon you!
We will live in God's wondrous light all our days!

Hymns

As With Gladness Men Of Old
Break Forth, O Beauteous Heavenly Light
Bright And Glorious Is The Sky
Brightest And Best Of The Stars Of The Morning
Go Tell It On The Mountain
Hail To The Brightness Of Zion's Glad Morning
I Want To Walk As A Child Of The Light
Shine, Jesus, Shine
Songs Of Thankfulness And Praise
We Three Kings Of Orient Are

Baptism of the Lord / First Sunday after the Epiphany / Ordinary Time 1

Isaiah 42:1-9
Psalm 29
Acts 10:34-43
Matthew 3:13-17

Call to Worship

Ascribe to the Lord glory and strength.
We give glory to the name of the Lord.

Worship the Lord in holy splendor.
Glory to God! Glory!

The Lord is enthroned over all creation.
The Lord will give us strength and bless us with peace.

Collect / Prayer of the Day

Great God, at the baptism of our Lord Jesus, you declared him your Son, the beloved, and your very Spirit descended upon him. By his baptism, life, death, and resurrection, make us, and all your children, to be faithful to our calling to live as your beloved daughters and sons, through Jesus Christ our Savior and Lord. Amen.

Confession / Assurance of Forgiveness

God says to you: "I am the Lord. I have called you in righteousness. I have taken you by the hand and kept you."
We give all our praise to the Lord our God.

We approach God openly and honestly, confessing our sin.
{silent prayer for personal confession of sins}

Creator God, we confess that, as your daughters and sons, we have sinned against you. We have rebelled against your holy will. We have not lived as responsible members of your family. We have selfishly judged others. We have ignored the pain and struggles of our sisters and brothers. Forgive us, and place within our hearts your forgiving, holy love. We ask that, with renewed hearts, your love will abide within and beyond us, through Jesus Christ our Lord. Amen.

Daughters and sons of God, believe this good news from God's own heart: in ✠ Jesus Christ, God forgives your sins.
Amen.

Prayers of the People / Prayers of Intercession

Gracious God, we give you thanks for the countless ways you make yourself known to us. Give us strength and wisdom to be good and faithful disciples of your Son. Hear us, O Lord.
Your mercy is great.

We pray for the church, that, by your Spirit, you would draw us together that we would be instruments to help make the world a more loving, just, and peaceful place for all your children. Hear us, O Lord.
Your mercy is great.

We pray for the people of every nation, that leaders would cooperate with each other to end violence, oppression, and the squandering of the life you give us. Hear us, O Lord.
Your mercy is great.

Bring peace to the world, our community, our families. Help us to end cruel behavior, bullying, and hurtful speech. Hear us, O Lord.
Your mercy is great.

Shape us, O God, to grow as disciples with holy integrity. Renew our vision that we would be your servants in our daily living. Draw us to yourself that we would live well-pleasing lives, as witnesses to your grace. Hear us, O Lord.
Your mercy is great.

We pray for your healing to come to those who are sick and suffering. *(Specific names are included here)*. Hear us, O Lord.
Your mercy is great.

As we remember those who have died, grant comfort and healing to all who grieve. Fill us with the light of the resurrection. Hear us, O Lord.
Your mercy is great.

Creator God, you called us in baptism, and you continue to call us every day. Hear our prayers and inspire us to listen for your voice, and live according to your will. In the name of Jesus.
Amen.

Sending Dialogue

Go forth to love and serve your neighbors.
We will travel, walking in love.

Care for one another and for the earth,
We will travel, bringing peace wherever we go.

Remember always that God goes before you.
We will travel, living confidently in God's grace.

Hymns

Baptized In Water
Christ, When For Us You Were Baptized
Come To Me, All Pilgrims Thirsty
God, When Human Bonds Are Broken
He Leadeth Me
Shall We Gather At The River
Songs Of Thankfulness And Praise
Wash, O God, Our Sons And Daughters
We Are Baptized In Christ Jesus
The Son Of Man From Jordan Rose

Second Sunday after the Epiphany / Ordinary Time 2

Isaiah 49:1-7
Psalm 40:1-11
1 Corinthians 1:1-9
John 1:29-42

Call to Worship
We gather to call on the name of our Lord, Jesus Christ.
Strengthen us, O God, with the spiritual gifts of your heart.

You are enriched in Christ, called into the fellowship of Christ Jesus.
God is faithful, from now until the end of the ages.

Grace to you and peace from God our Father and the Lord Jesus Christ.
We give thanks to God for the grace that we receive.

Collect / Prayer of the Day
Almighty God, in Christ you make all things new. Send down your Spirit upon us and remain with us always. Sanctify us and grant us your grace and peace. Enrich us in speech, in knowledge, in daily living. Strengthen us with spiritual gifts. Keep us in your love. We pray in the name of the Lamb of God, Jesus our Lord. Amen.

Confession / Assurance of Forgiveness
Give thanks to the Lord, for God is good.
God's steadfast love endures forever.

Let us confess our sin before our God of love.
{silent prayer for personal confession of sins}

God of steadfast love, forgive us for half-hearted discipleship. Forgive us when we distort your word. Forgive us for the times we have disregarded your commandments. Forgive us our every sin. Give us joy, determination, and courage to follow you in word and deed. Make us new and prepare us to be your servants. In the holy name of Jesus, we pray. Amen.

The grace of God has been given to you in Christ Jesus. As you receive Christ, so live in him. Receive now, once again, divine grace. Receive divine strength. Receive the forgiveness of your sins, through the faithfulness of ✠ Jesus Christ our Lord.
Amen.

Prayers of the People / Prayers of Intercession

Hear us, O loving God, as we pray for all the people of the earth. Send your Spirit into the world to inspire everyone to experience your love. Unite us in your truth and grace, and let your divine love shine through us to others. God of love,
Hear our prayer.

Empower your church on earth to lovingly, patiently, and with holy speech proclaim your saving work to all the world. God of love,
Hear our prayer.

We pray for our nation, and all the nations of the world, that each citizen would choose to live in peace, kindness, and love for others. Purge prejudices, hatefulness, and greed from those who embrace these transgressions. God of love,
Hear our prayer.

Let your Spirit of forgiveness, joy, and love enter our families. May your divine presence be the foundation of every relationship, of every home. Embrace the lonely with your presence. God of love,
Hear our prayer.

Embrace the deeply hurt and the angry with your grace. In your compassion, send them your love through caring and patient disciples. God of love,
Hear our prayer.

We pray for your healing graces upon all who are sick in body, mind, and spirit. *(Specific names are included here)*. God of love,
Hear our prayer.

As we are called to be saints on earth, we remember the saints in heaven and rejoice in the resurrection. Be merciful to those who grieve. God of love,
Hear our prayer.

Holy God, we trust that you are eternally faithful to all your children. With confidence, we place all our prayers, spoken and unspoken, into your hands, in the name of Jesus, our Lord.
Amen.

Sending Dialogue

You have heard the word of God.
We will live in fellowship with Jesus Christ our Lord.

Do not grow weary of doing what is right.
We will live in God's love and in grace.

Walk daily with Christ Jesus.
We will follow him and serve in his name.

Hymns

Arise, Your Light Is Come!
As With Gladness Men Of Old
Hope Of The World
I Lay My Sins On Jesus
I Love To Tell The Story
Jesus Calls Us, O'er The Tumult
Jesus Shall Reign
Just As I Am, Without One Plea
Lamb Of God (Your Only Son)
O God, Our Help In Ages Past

Third Sunday after the Epiphany / Ordinary Time 3

Isaiah 9:1-4
Psalm 27:1, 4-9
1 Corinthians 1:10-18
Matthew 4:12-23

Call to Worship
The Lord is my light and my salvation.
The Lord is the stronghold of my life.

God will shelter me in the day of trouble.
God will protect me and lift me high.

We will sing and make melody to the Lord.
We will praise the Lord in joy and in gladness.

Collect / Prayer of the Day
Holy God, you have called us through Christ Jesus to proclaim the good news of the kingdom with the gifts you have given us. Lead us out of darkness into your divine light. Guide us to live according to your word. Unite us in the name of Jesus Christ, our Lord. Amen.

Confession / Assurance of Forgiveness
Jesus proclaimed, "Repent, for the kingdom of heaven has come near."
The kingdom of heaven is near to us now.

We approach God's throne of grace with repentant hearts.
{silent prayer for personal confession of sins}

Almighty God, we confess that we have lived in darkness. We have tuned out the cries of those who are hurting. We have failed to nourish the hungry. We have covered our ears to the call to follow Jesus. We have created divisions in our stubbornness. We have failed in the ways of unity and peaceful living. Because of your grace, we trust, Lord, that you will not forsake us. You will not turn us away. Forgive us and fill us with the power of your salvation, in Christ our Lord. Amen.

Hear the good news: God has not and will not turn you away. God will never forsake you. God, in ✠ Jesus Christ, forgives your sins. Rejoice and trust in the light of God's love.
Amen.

Prayers of the People / Prayers of Intercession

Loving God, bring unity to the church. By your Holy Spirit, guide all believers and leaders to seek unity, rather than division and separation from one another. Lord, hear our prayer.
Have mercy on us and answer us.

Guide our national, regional, and local government leaders, and the leaders of all nations, to dedicate themselves to the welfare of their people and make decisions for the common good. Lord, hear our prayer.
Have mercy on us and answer us.

We pray for the weakest and most vulnerable among us, for the hungry and homeless, the lonely and the unemployed, those who live in fear and those who live without faith and love. Make us good stewards to answer your call to care for them. Make us loving instruments of all the gifts you have given us. Lord, hear our prayer.
Have mercy on us and answer us.

We pray for missionaries throughout the world, and for believers who are persecuted for their faith. Protect and shelter them in your loving care. Lord, hear our prayer.
Have mercy on us and answer us.

Inspire this congregation that we may be a model of unity and mutual care for one another. Unite us in mind and purpose. Bind us together as a loving community of believers. Lord, hear our prayer.
Have mercy on us and answer us.

Remembering how Jesus, your Son, was among us in Galilee, teaching, proclaiming good news, and curing every disease and sickness among the people, we pray now for the sick, and all those who cry out for your care. *(Specific names are included here).* Lord, hear our prayer.
Have mercy on us and answer us.

Remembering our loved ones who have died, we give thanks for the message of the cross, the power of our salvation. Grant this power and holy comfort to all who grieve, that we may be filled with the joy of your salvation. Lord, hear our prayer.
Have mercy on us and answer us.

God of our salvation, you are present with us now in Jesus Christ. We trust that you hear and answer us. Send forth your light to drive the darkness from our lives, in the holy name of Jesus.
Amen.

Sending Dialogue

Darkness will not overcome us.
The Lord is our light.

God's light illuminates our path.
Christ Jesus shines within us all.

Do not grow weary of leading others to God's kingdom.
We will follow Jesus and the example he has given us.

Hymns

Come, Follow Me, The Savior Spake
I Lay My Sins On Jesus
Jesus Calls Us; O'er The Tumult
Lift High The Cross
O Jesus, Joy Of Loving Hearts
O Master, Let Me Walk With You
The Voice Of God Is Calling
Thine Is The Glory
Will You Come And Follow Me? (The Summons)
You Have Come Down To The Lakeshore

Fourth Sunday after the Epiphany / Ordinary Time 4

Micah 6:1-8
Psalm 15
1 Corinthians 1:18-31
Matthew 5:1-12

Call to Worship
By the call of the Holy Spirit, we gather to praise God.
Blessed are we when we receive new life in Christ.

God's word is our delight.
God's word is a lamp to my feet and a light to my path.

We are called to love and serve others in Christ's name.
We live in God's reign now and forever.

Collect / Prayer of the Day
Merciful God, your gift of life brings us joy. When we trust in your goodness, you give us strength. You have chosen us, even in our weakness, to follow your Son. By your grace, you are saving us through the power of his cross. Send us your Holy Spirit, that we would become people of justice and kindness, humbly walking with you daily. We pray in the name of Jesus Christ our Lord. Amen.

Confession / Assurance of Forgiveness
The message of the cross is foolishness to those who are perishing.
To us who are being saved, the cross is the power of God.

We confess that we have embraced the foolishness of sin.
{silent prayer for personal confession of sins}

God on high, we confess that we have sought to be blessed by the things of the world. We have embraced the ways of this age. We have ignored, even disbelieved, your image in others. We have walked away from you. Forgive us for not trusting in you, in your ways, in your will. Grant us the blessings again of being your children and give us the true joy that will remain within us forever. We pray in Jesus' name. Amen.

In the wisdom and grace of God, we receive life, blessings galore, and forgiveness. I proclaim that this is God's will for you. Receive now, life, blessings, and forgiveness, in the name of ✠ Jesus Christ our Lord.
Amen.

Prayers of the People / Prayers of Intercession

God who walks with us, we pray that the church on earth would live your holy word day after day. Inspire us to be holy. Grant your blessings upon those who preach, those who make beautiful music, those who pray, teach, counsel, comfort, and reach out in service to those in need. God of life,
Bless us and hear our prayer.

Bless the leaders of every nation and all who serve in public office. Grant them holy energy, wisdom, and dedication to serve the common good. We pray they walk with you humbly. Inspire them to turn away from the absurdity of sin and evil. God of life,
Bless us and hear our prayer.

Send ministers of healing and caring to those without nourishing food, fresh water, adequate shelter, or access to medical care. Be present with those who lack hope. God of life,
Bless us and hear our prayer.

Send your divine care to those who are held captive by the darkness of doubt, the pain of depression, the struggle of lacking faith, or the hurt of low self-worth. Bless them, embrace them, love them with your everlasting love. God of life,
Bless us and hear our prayer.

We pray for the well-being of your creation. Where the earth is in distress, protect and rescue all who struggle, all those in danger, all who are suffering. Grant courage and strength to those who work to serve and protect those in danger. God of life,
Bless us and hear our prayer.

We pray for those who are sick and in distress, for those who suffer in any way. *(Specific names are included here)*. God of life,
Bless us and hear our prayer.

We pray for those who grieve. Grant your blessings upon their memories, their tears, their laughter. Embrace them with your resurrection-love. God of life,
Bless us and hear our prayer.

Loving and compassionate God, hear the prayers we offer today, in the name of Jesus our Lord.
Amen.

Sending Dialogue

We go forth into our world as the children of God.
We will serve others by the grace of God.

We go with the grace of the Lord, Jesus Christ.
We will bring God's grace, peace, and forgiveness into the world.

We are abundantly blessed people!
We will walk daily with Jesus Christ our Lord.

Hymns

Be Thou My Vision
Blest Are the Humble Souls That See
Canticle Of The Turning
Give To Our God Immortal Praise!
He Leadeth Me
Let The Whole Creation Cry
Let Us Ever Walk With Jesus
Lord, Whose Love In Humble Service
Many Are The Lightbeams
We Are The Light Of The World

Fifth Sunday after the Epiphany / Ordinary Time 5

Isaiah 58:1-9a [9b-12]
Psalm 112:1-9 [10]
1 Corinthians 2:1-12 [13-16]
Matthew 5:13-20

Call to Worship
Lift up your voice to the Lord!
Praise the Lord, who is our light!

Lift up your heart to the Lord!
Praise the Lord, who guides us continually!

Lift up your life to the Lord!
Praise the Lord, who blesses the upright!

Collect / Prayer of the Day
Creator God, make us channels of the light you have created. Shine the light of your Son through our lives and into the whole world, that kindness, love, compassion, and forgiveness abound in all places, and at all times, in and through Jesus Christ, the light of the world. Amen.

Confession / Assurance of Forgiveness
We have not received the spirit of the world.
We have received the Holy Spirit that is from God.

Embraced by this very Spirit, we confess our sins before God.
{silent prayer for personal confession of sins}

God of mercy and truth, we confess that we have sometimes allowed darkness to touch our lives through hatefulness, prejudices, hateful words, hateful thoughts, anger in relationships, gossip, destroying the reputation of others, lack of respect for others, injuring the self-esteem of others, treating people in unholy ways. Forgive us, O God, forgive us. Give us the mind of Christ, the heart of Christ, the Spirit of Christ. In his holy name we pray. Amen.

As you have recognized the foolishness of your sins, know this: God does not reject you because you have been foolish, selfish, or sinful. No, God embraces you, loves you, and gives you the divine nourishment of grace and love. God forgives you, through ✠ Jesus Christ our Lord.
Amen.

Prayers of the People / Prayers of Intercession

Holy God, reach down and embrace your church on earth, and make the church become salt and light for others. Form the fellowship of believers into a beautiful city, doing good work that gives you glory. God of light,
Hear our prayer.

Reach down and embrace the nations and leaders of the world. Bestow your gifts upon them that they would reject violent, destructive, and sinful ways. God of light,
Hear our prayer.

Reach down and embrace those who are powerless, unloved, rejected, and oppressed. Strengthen them in your persevering love. God of light,
Hear our prayer.

Reach down and embrace those in despair, those who struggle with doubt, unbelief, and guilt. Place on their hearts your loving grace and compassion. God of light,
Hear our prayer.

Reach down and embrace those who are being strangled by anxiety, grief, and fear. Be present with them and let them experience your holy presence. God of light,
Hear our prayer.

Reach down and embrace those who are sick. Shine your healing light upon them. *(Specific names are included here)*. God of light,
Hear our prayer.

Reach down and lovingly embrace the dying. Grant them stillness of soul, calmness of heart, and a mindful assurance of your resurrection. God of light,
Hear our prayer.

God of our salvation, receive these and all our prayers, through the light of the world, Jesus Christ, our Savior.
Amen.

Sending Dialogue

You are the salt of the earth.
We will season the world with God's love.

You are the light of the world.
We will teach and live the commandments of the Lord.

You are a city on a hill.
We will let the goal and purpose of our good works be the glory to God.

Hymns

Arise, Your Light Is Come
Christ, Be Our Light
Blessing And Honor
Go, My Children, With My Blessing
O Word Of God Incarnate
Rise, Shine, You People!
Sent Forth By God's Blessing
This Little Light Of Mine
Thy Strong Word
We Eat The Bread Of Teaching

Sixth Sunday after the Epiphany / Proper 1 / Ordinary Time 6

Deuteronomy 30:15-20
Psalm 119:1-8
1 Corinthians 3:1-9
Matthew 5:21-3

Call to Worship

Come, let us give praise to God!
We praise our God who gives us life.

Come, let us lift our hearts to the God of glory!
We worship our God who lifts us high.

Come, let us sing to the goodness of God!
We listen to the word and accept the will of God.

Collect / Prayer of the Day

Merciful God, you have given us life itself, commandments to follow, and nourishment to keep us strong. As we hear your word and commands once again, grant us your Holy Spirit, and open our ears and our hearts to hear you with clarity and openness. Strengthen us to renew our commitment to live according to the teachings of your Son, Jesus Christ, our Lord. Amen.

Confession / Assurance of Forgiveness

Create in me a clean heart, O God.
Renew a right spirit within me.

Let us make a commitment to renewal, choosing the life that God offers us. As we do, we confess the times we have failed to embrace God's life, the times we have sinned.
{silent prayer for personal confession of sins}

God of life, you have set before us the way of life by the life, death, and resurrection of your Son. But we have not always chosen to accept the call. We have been blinded by our self-centered decisions. We have not been thankful for your life-giving gifts. We have not fixed our eyes on your commandments. We have not sought to be reconciled with our sisters and brothers. Forgive us. Restore us. Renew us. Do not forsake us. Cleanse us from our sins. We pray in the name of Jesus. Amen.

God's light shines in the darkness. God's love is eternally steadfast. God's heart is a forgiving heart. I therefore proclaim that God is now forgiving you your sins, for the sake of ✠ Jesus Christ our Savior and Lord.
Amen.

Prayers of the People / Prayers of Intercession

Merciful and holy God, cast out those things which separate us from you and from one another. Unite us and restore our wounded and broken relationships. God, in your mercy,
Hear our prayer.

Be with us through those times when we face fear, fatigue, and failure. Protect and strengthen us in your grace. God, in your mercy,
Hear our prayer.

We pray for all the expressions of the church, for bishops, pastors, lay leaders, missionaries, and all believers working in the church. Strengthen and guide us to care for the poor, the hungry, the thirsty, and all those who struggle. God, in your mercy,
Hear our prayer.

We pray for all those who govern, that they act according to your ways of freedom and peace. Grant them your wisdom and compassion. Pour out your peace upon all the nations. God, in your mercy,
Hear our prayer.

We pray for the children in our families and for all children everywhere. We pray for their safety and well-being. Protect the children, O God, and grant healing and love to those who have been exploited and injured by sin and evil. God, in your mercy,
Hear our prayer.

Give light and healing to those surrounded by the darkness of illness or grief. Ease their pain and restore them to health. *(Specific names are included here)*. God, in your mercy,
Hear our prayer.

Hold us in communion with all the faithful witnesses who have gone before us, until that day when you unite us all in heaven. God, in your mercy,
Hear our prayer.

God of healing, you call your people to show your endless love to others. Give us the courage to live as we are called, that we would reflect your light to those who sit in darkness. We ask this in the name of Jesus, light of the world.
Amen.

Sending Dialogue

We are God's servants.
We will work together as God assigns and directs us.

We are God's field.
We will plant and water according to God's purpose.

We are God's building.
We will dwell together in the heart of God's love.

Hymns

Forgive Our Sins As We Forgive
Give Me Jesus
God, When Human Bonds Are Broken
Great Is Thy Faithfulness
Jesus Loves Me!
Joyful, Joyful We Adore Thee
Lord, Take My Hand And Lead Me
O Day Of Rest And Gladness
Oh, Sing To The Lord
Take My Life, That I May Be

Seventh Sunday after the Epiphany / Proper 2 / Ordinary Time 7

Leviticus 19:1-2, 9-18
Psalm 119:33-40
1 Corinthians 3:10-11, 16-23
Matthew 5:38-48

Call to Worship

Teach us, O Lord, your ways.
We delight in the ways of God.

Lead me, O Lord, in the path of your commandments.
We delight in the teachings of God.

We gather in the name of the Lord God, who is holy.
We belong to Christ. We live in Christ, now and always.

Collect / Prayer of the Day

God of love, we are your temple, holy, set apart from worldly, sinful ways. As the church, we belong to each other. We belong to Christ. Draw us together, mold us, and connect us to one another through your Holy Spirit. Teach us your ways of love and compassion. Unite us as your children who desire to follow your Son, our Lord and Savior, Jesus Christ. Amen.

Confession / Assurance of Forgiveness

I am the Lord your God. You, my people, shall be holy.
You are our God. We will love you, and we will love our neighbor as ourselves.

We confess our sins as a family of faith.
{silent prayer for personal confession of sins}

God, our great redeemer, according to your will for us, we have not always loved you, we have not always loved our neighbor, we have not always loved ourselves. We have not always accepted your call to love our enemies. We have failed to pray for those who persecute us. We have failed to be generous. We have not gone the extra mile. Forgive us, Lord, for all of our sinful, selfish ways. Fill us with the desire to hear and heed your word, and to remember to whom we belong, Jesus Christ our Lord. Amen.

Rejoice! As we confess our sins and repent, our Lord has promised to forgive us. God is faithful and just. God is merciful and loving. God is forgiving your sins, in the name of the Father, ✠ Son, and Holy Spirit.
Amen.

Prayers of the People / Prayers of Intercession

O Light of the world, we praise, adore, and thank you for the light you shine upon us and among us. We ask you this day to illuminate us as we journey. Direct us away from darkness, sin, and the ways of destruction. Let your glory, your love, and your grace shine forth by the way we live. God of grace,
Hear our prayer.

Guide your whole church on earth to live the ways of love. Remove all deceit, hypocrisy, and division among us. Teach us to not boast in ourselves, but to lift up the glory of your name. Make us holy and loving. God of grace,
Hear our prayer.

Let your blessings rest upon the nations and upon the leaders of the nations. Draw this world away from the paths of war, oppression, terrorism, hatefulness, and violence. Soften hardened hearts and open them to your ways of love. God of grace,
Hear our prayer.

Prepare us to receive your divine and heavenly gifts, and direct us to use them to meet the needs of your children. Bless and multiply your gifts. God of grace,
Hear our prayer.

Grant us gentleness and patience in our teaching, so that children and youth, and those new to the faith, will clearly hear the goodness of your commands, and that your grace and blessings will embrace their lives. God of grace,
Hear our prayer.

Grant healing to the sick and suffering. Return them to wellness and let your glory shine in their lives. *(Specific names are included here)*. God of grace,
Hear our prayer.

Grant resurrection-light to those who grieve. Bless their memories with peace, forgiveness, and love. God of grace,
Hear our prayer.

Holy God, hear these our prayers, and the prayers of all your children. Let the brightness of your redemption shine in the world, and in our daily lives, through Jesus Christ, our Lord.
Amen.

Sending Dialogue

May the teachings of our Lord Jesus Christ abide in you and guide you.
We will abide in Christ, and we will teach God's love.

May the love of our Lord Jesus Christ strengthen you in daily living.
We will love others in Christ, and we will serve in his name.

May the resurrection-joy of our Lord Jesus Christ overflow in your hearts, minds, and souls.
We will rejoice in Christ, and we will witness to God's grace.

Hymns

Blest Be The Tie That Binds
Dear Lord And Father Of Mankind
God Of Grace And God Of Glory
Gracious Spirit, Dwell With Me
Great God, We Sing Your Mighty Hand
Holy, Holy, Holy! Lord God Almighty!
Immortal, Invisible, God Only Wise
In Christ There Is No East Or West
O God Of Earth And Altar
We Would Be Building

Transfiguration Sunday / Last Sunday after the Epiphany

Those who don't observe Transfiguration Sunday, should use:
Ninth Sunday after the Epiphany [Proper 4, Ordinary Time 9]

Exodus 24:12-18
Psalm 2 or Psalm 99
2 Peter 1:16-21
Matthew 17:1-9

Call to Worship

Exalt the Lord our God, and worship at God's holy mountain.
Glory be to God, who is holy and majestic. Alleluia!

The brilliance of the glory of God is revealed in Jesus.
Glory be to God, who loves us and calls us by name. Alleluia!

We gather to hear the voice of God.
Glory be to God, who speaks to us and gives us ears to hear. Alleluia!

Collect / Prayer of the Day

God of glory, you reveal yourself to us through the life, death, and resurrection of Jesus. As the apostles of old saw your glory, reveal yourself to us in our day. Come to us in love, sustain us by your mercy, renew us by your grace, through your beloved Son, Jesus Christ, our Lord and Savior. Amen.

Confession / Assurance of Forgiveness

The glory of the Lord endures forever. Alleluia!
We will praise the Lord all our days. Alleluia!

Together we seek the forgiveness of our loving and gracious God.
{silent prayer for personal confession of sins}

Mighty and eternal God, we come before you with humble hearts, confessing our sins, acknowledging our weaknesses. We confess that we have taken your presence in our lives for granted. We have served our own purposes, ignoring your will. We have failed to cherish all your children. We have failed to be channels of your light and glory. Break into our hearts, O God, reveal your majestic love to us, and open us to your majesty. Forgive us. Heal us. Shine your heavenly light upon us, through Jesus our Lord. Amen.

Hear good news: you are a beloved child of God. Do not be afraid of the one who comes to you in heavenly love and eternal power. God forgives you through ✠ Jesus Christ, God's Son, the beloved.
Amen. Alleluia! Amen.

Prayers of the People / Prayers of Intercession

Holy God, holy, mighty, holy and immortal, transfigure your church, that we may bring the light and life of your beloved Son into the whole world. God of glory,
Hear our prayer.

Give the leaders of all nations a vision of the world at peace. Inspire them to work together for the welfare of all people. God of glory,
Hear our prayer.

Almighty God, as our Lord Jesus led the apostles down from the mountaintop to continue their journey, keep us in footstep with Jesus that we might become teachers of the good news, healers, care-givers, and witnesses to the mystery of your Son's sacrificial love. God of glory,
Hear our prayer.

Renew the earth's waters, lands, and skies to reflect your glory. Guide us to be respectful in our use of the earthly resources you have provided for us. God of glory,
Hear our prayer.

Enlighten missionaries and give strength to care-giving ministers. Let your glory shine through their actions, words, and works of mercy. God of glory,
Hear our prayer.

Give light and healing to all who are living with the darkness of suffering in body, mind, heart, or spirit. *(Specific names are included here).* God of glory,
Hear our prayer.

We give thanks for all the beloved who eternally rest in your loving arms. Keep us strong on our journey and strengthen our faith in your promise of everlasting life. God of glory,
Hear our prayer.

Lord God, heal our broken and hurting world with your light, glory, and grace. Transform your children to live in your light and to show forth your glory. As we cry out to you, O Lord, answer us, in Jesus' holy name.
Amen.

Sending Dialogue

Be attentive to the presence of God in your daily living.
The love and glory of God the Father will go with us. Alleluia!

Let God's light shine in every dark place you encounter.
The grace of our Lord Jesus Christ will strengthen us. Alleluia!

Take refuge in God and walk daily with Jesus, serving in his name.
The power of the Holy Spirit will lead and guide us. Alleluia!

Hymns

Alleluia, Song Of Gladness
Beautiful Savior
Blessing And Honor
Christ, Whose Glory Fills The Skies
How Good, Lord, To Be Here!
I Know My Redeemer Lives!
Immortal, Invisible, God Only Wise
Praise, My Soul, The God Of Heaven
Shine, Jesus, Shine
To God Be The Glory

Ash Wednesday

Joel 2:1-2, 12-17 or Isaiah 58:1-12
Psalm 51:1-17
2 Corinthians 5:20b–6:10
Matthew 6:1-6, 16-21

Call to Worship
Seek the Lord while God may be found.
We call upon our God who is near.

Rend your hearts, not your garments.
Create in me a clean heart, O God, and put a new and right spirit within me.

All praise to God, through our Lord Jesus Christ.
We will turn to the Lord, our God, who is gracious and merciful, slow to anger, and abounding in steadfast love.

Collect / Prayer of the Day
Merciful God, it is the desire of our souls to be reconciled with you. This is the proper time to repent and turn to you for grace and forgiveness. Open our hearts and minds to accept your will, to follow in your ways, and to receive your grace. We turn to you for mercy, generous and forgiving God, through Christ our Lord. Amen.

Confession / Assurance of Forgiveness
Create in me a clean heart, O God.
Put a new and right spirit within me.

Turn to God now, confessing your sins.
{silent prayer for personal confession of sins}

Most holy and merciful God, we confess to you that we have sinned against you, and against our sisters and brothers, your children. We have not loved you. We have not served our neighbor. We have not been forgiving and generous. We have placed obstacles in the ways of holiness and righteousness. We have been proud, hypocritical, impatient, self-indulgent. We have been unfaithful. Lord, have mercy on us. Amen.

Through the power of Christ Jesus, in your repentance and trust, God releases you from the bondage and guilt of your sins. By the cross and resurrection, God sets you free in ✠ Jesus Christ, our Lord.
Amen.

Prayers of the People / Prayers of Intercession

Loving God, bless us as we begin a new Lenten journey, a new season of repentance and reflection. Give us the strength of your Son, who prayed in Gethsemane, "Thy will be done." Loving God,
Hear our prayer.

Lay your blessings upon us this Lenten Season. Help us to focus on Jesus, that we may serve as examples of your holy ways. Fill our hearts with your Holy Spirit that, as disciples, we would reflect the love of Jesus in our daily living. Loving God,
Hear our prayer.

Grant us the strength of endurance in our day, strength in times of affliction, hardship, calamities, sleepless nights. Embrace us with your grace. Inspire church and civic leaders to lead according to your will. Loving God,
Hear our prayer.

By your Holy Spirit, give us an overflowing measure of patience, kindness, holiness of spirit, genuine love, truthful speech. Loving God,
Hear our prayer.

We pray for those in the world who are living in deep darkness and gloom. We pray for those who are weeping and grieving, those who are lost, lonely, abused, oppressed. Bring them into your presence and grant them healing. Send ministers and missionaries to care for them in loving and holy ways. Loving God,
Hear our prayer.

We humbly pray to you, even beg you, to grant healing and mercy to those who are sick, suffering, and struggling. Give them assurance of your constant and abiding love. *(Specific names are included here)*. Loving God,
Hear our prayer.

As we have commended to your care our loved ones who have passed from this life into that greater light and life you have prepared for your servants, assure our hearts, minds, and souls of your glorious resurrection. Loving God,
Hear our prayer.

We lift our prayers to you, God of grace and truth. Receive them in your mercy, and grant us all that we need, in Jesus' name.
Amen.

Sending Dialogue

As you go forth, be reconciled with God, in Christ Jesus.
We will live so that our hearts and souls will remain joined to God.

Accept and receive the grace of God now and in the season ahead.
We will, and we will work together as servants in God's kingdom.

Store up for yourselves treasures in heaven.
As often as we receive the treasures of God, we will speak and act to reflect God's grace in the world.

Hymns

Abide With Me
Chief Of Sinners Though I Be
Christ, The Life Of All The Living
I Lay My Sins On Jesus
Just As I Am, Without One Plea
Lord Jesus, Think On Me
O Lord, Throughout These Forty Days
On My Heart Imprint Your Image
Softly And Tenderly Jesus Is Calling
What Wondrous Love Is This?

First Sunday in Lent

Genesis 2:15-17; 3:1-7
Psalm 32
Romans 5:12-19
Matthew 4:1-11

Call to Worship
The Lord will be a hiding place for us and preserve us from trouble.
We will worship the Lord our God.

The Lord will counsel you with an eye upon you.
We will serve only the Lord our God.

The Lord will instruct you and teach you the way you should go.
We will live by every word that comes from the mouth of God.

Collect / Prayer of the Day
Lord our God, we call upon you in these days of darkness, thirst, and temptation. Strengthen us to rely on the cross of your Son, Jesus Christ. Empower us to refrain from building walls of sin. Inspire us by your holy word to resist and overcome temptations. Transform us and renew us to live in accordance with your will. In Jesus' name we pray. Amen.

Confession / Assurance of Forgiveness
Blessed are those whose sins are forgiven by God.
I will confess my transgressions to the Lord.

Let us now acknowledge our sin before the Lord.
{silent prayer for personal confession of sins}

Gracious God, we pray for your mercy and forgiveness. Forgive us for the brokenness of our lives caused by our sins. Forgive is when we surrendered to temptation. Forgive our excessive reliance on material things of the world. Forgive our coldness of heart to those in need. Forgive our inattention to your presence in our lives. Forgive us when we have neglected your laws and precepts, especially your command to love as your Son has loved us. Change our hearts, O God, that we would cling to your abundant and overflowing grace, through Jesus Christ our Lord. Amen.

"Blessed are those whose sins are forgiven by God. Blessed are those whose sin is wiped away." Friends in Christ, trust in God's word. Rejoice and be glad. Through God's word, I announce that God is forgiving you your sins, through ✠ Jesus Christ our Lord. **Amen.**

Prayers of the People / Prayers of Intercession

God who listens to our every prayer, we thank you that you come to us with light and are with us when darkness surrounds us. We thank you for Jesus Christ, his redemptive work, his teachings, and the example he gives us for living in this world. Lord, in your mercy,
Hear our prayer.

Guard your church from falling when temptations arise. Restore your church in times of failure. When needed, guide your church to repent. Restore and form your church again into your chosen people. Lord, in your mercy,
Hear our prayer.

We pray for the nations of world, especially when nation fights against nation. Take away the desire to lift the sword and engage in war. Inspire leaders in every form of government to lead your children into your ways of peace and justice. Lord, in your mercy,
Hear our prayer.

We pray for those who suffer because of war, homelessness, hunger and thirst, injustice, oppression, all attacks of the devil. We pray that your free gift of grace be more and more embraced in the world. Lord, in your mercy,
Hear our prayer.

We pray for those who work for the well-being of others, for health-care workers, first responders, teachers, missionaries, and every caregiver. Strengthen and prosper them in their work. Lord, in your mercy,
Hear our prayer.

We pray for those who are sick, afflicted in body and mind, distressed by pain and suffering. Heal, comfort, and protect them. *(Specific names are included here)*. Lord, in your mercy,
Hear our prayer.

Remembering loved ones who have died, grant your tender care to all who struggle with grief. Grant the grieving ones the bread of heaven, divine living water, and an abundance of resurrection-light. Lord, in your mercy,
Hear our prayer.

God of salvation, hear our prayers and grant your blessing to all people. Free us from every evil, that we may serve you in peace and joy, through Jesus Christ our Lord.
Amen.

Sending Dialogue

As you go out into the garden of your life, walk with God.
We will walk with God daily, wherever we go.

As you travel the wilderness of temptation, receive the Holy Spirit.
We will resist temptations with the very power of God's word.

As you re-enter a world of transgressions and sin, go with the grace of God.
We will be open to the abundance of grace that God will send to us in Christ.

Hymns

A Mighty Fortress Is Our God
Bless Now, O God, The Journey
Guide Me Ever, Great Redeemer
I Want Jesus To Walk With Me
Lead On, O King Eternal!
My Faith Looks Up To Thee
On Eagle's Wings
The Glory Of These Forty Days
Through The Night Of Doubt And Sorrow
When Peace, Like A River

Second Sunday in Lent

For those who don't observe Transfiguration Sunday the week before Lent, use: Matthew 17:1-9 for the Gospel.

Genesis 12:1-4a
Psalm 121
Romans 4:1-5, 13-17
John 3:1-17

Call to Worship

Trust in God with all your heart, soul, and mind.
We trust Jesus who was lifted up to draw all people to himself.

Indeed, the Son of Man was lifted up, that whoever believes in him may have eternal life.
God so loved the world that he gave his only Son, so that everyone who believes in him may not perish, but may have eternal life.

God did not send the Son into the world to condemn the world. **God sent the Son in order that the world might be saved through him.**

Collect / Prayer of the Day

Saving God, the cross of your Son was an instrument of suffering, shame, and death. But, by your eternal power, his cross has become our salvation, our redemption, our eternal life. Grant us your Holy Spirit to keep our hearts centered on this instrument of your grace. Draw us, and all people, into the presence of Jesus, Savior of the world, now, always, and forever. Amen.

Confession / Assurance of Forgiveness

No one can see the kingdom of God without being born from above.
You must be born from above.

Thinking about our new birth in Christ, we confess our sins, that we might embrace the forgiveness of God with integrity.
{silent prayer for personal confession of sins}

God of life, you are with us always, and yet we ignore, even reject your presence. We fail to trust in you. We live as foolish, lost, and faithless children. Forgive us these and all our private, personal sins. Fill us with the faith of Jesus. Raise us up in the Spirit from above. Have mercy on us. Amen.

People of God, there is abundant, divine mercy for you. There is mercy in the new birth from above. There is mercy in the confession of sins. There is mercy in a daily willingness to be reborn from above. There is mercy in the cross of Christ. Rejoice! Rejoice in God's eternal love, in God's forgiveness, in new life. God forgives you in ✠ Jesus Christ the suffering servant, the one who is forever alive and present.
Amen.

Prayers of the People / Prayers of Intercession

Gracious Lord God, we praise and thank you for your generous, forgiving love, which gives us growth and strength for daily living. Gracious Lord,
Hear our prayer.

We pray for rebirth in the church, for renewal of spirit, for generosity in forgiving, for your blessings upon the church's teaching, learning, and listening. Help us to be attentive to your word. Gracious Lord,
Hear our prayer.

We pray for rebirth among the nations, that world and local leaders would work diligently to provide food for the hungry, freedom for the oppressed, and peace for those living in fear. Gracious Lord,
Hear our prayer.

We pray for renewal in families, that relationships would be loving, that your children would affirm and love one another. Inspire us to put away self-centeredness, prejudice, and hateful actions. Gracious Lord,
Hear our prayer.

We pray for schools, for all students, teachers, administrators, staff, parents, and caregivers. As you are ever-present with them, bless them with in your care. Encourage and sustain them every day by your divine love. Gracious Lord,
Hear our prayer.

Grant healing to those who suffer in body, mind, or spirit. Strengthen those who are weak. *(Specific names are included here).* Gracious Lord,
Hear our prayer.

Give deep peace to those near death, comfort those who grieve, and renew us all in our faith in eternal life. Gracious Lord,
Hear our prayer.

Healing God, have mercy on us and hear our prayers. Warm our hearts daily with the light of your loving grace, through Jesus Christ our Lord.
Amen.

Sending Dialogue

Go now into the world to bear witness to the redeeming love of God.
We go with strengthened faith.

Go now with open hearts, open to new directions of service, witness, and growth.
We go with renewed hope.

Go now to be a blessing to others, trusting in the guidance of the Holy Spirit.
We go, reborn with God's love.

Hymns

Depth Of Mercy
God Loved The World
Jesus, Keep Me Near The Cross
Jesus Loves Me!
Lift High The Cross
My Faith Looks Up To Thee
My Hope Is Built On Nothing Less
O Love Divine, What Hast Thou Done
Stand Up, Stand Up For Jesus
You Are My Hiding Place

Third Sunday in Lent

Exodus 17:1-7
Psalm 95
Romans 5:1-11
John 4:5-42

Call to Worship

Come, let us sing to the Lord.
We will make a joyful noise to the rock of our salvation.

We gather in God's presence with thanksgiving.
We make a joyful noise to God with songs of praise.

O that today you would listen to God's voice.
We will not harden your hearts. We will embrace God's ways.

Collect / Prayer of the Day

God of life, you offer living water to your children. We gather today to drink deeply of all that you offer us. Renew us, transform us, and give us the desire to share your provisions of grace with all who are thirsty. We pray in the name of the one who is truly the Savior of the world, Jesus Christ, our Lord. Amen.

Confession / Assurance of Forgiveness

Let us humble ourselves before God our Maker.
As we bow down and worship, we proclaim: the Lord alone is our God.

Let us confess our sin before God and one another.
{silent prayer for personal confession of sins}

God, our God, we confess that we have not always done your will. We have broken your law. We have hardened our hearts. We have rebelled against you. Like sheep, we have gone astray. We have ignored the cries of those in need and refused to share your gifts with our neighbor. Forgive us, cleanse us, restore us. We ask in the name of Jesus. Amen.

God hears our requests. As we ask, God's love is being poured into our hearts through the Holy Spirit. While we were still weak, while we were still sinners, Christ died for us. Now, we are reconciled to God through the death of Jesus, and we are being saved by his life. God is forgiving you through our Lord ✠ Jesus Christ.
Amen.

Prayers of the People / Prayers of Intercession

God, our great provider, we thank and praise you that you nourish us with divine food and living water for our souls. Remind us daily to eat and drink deeply of your love. By your Spirit, remind us to invite others to receive your gifts. God our provider,
Hear our prayer.

Make your church a vessel of your wisdom, understanding, nourishment, and love, that people would be drawn to receive what you offer. God our provider,
Hear our prayer.

Grant peace to our world, to all nations, to all peoples. By your grace, soften hardened hearts of leaders, judges, lawmakers, and citizens. Keep us from the dangers of war, oppression, and violence. Reconcile nation to nation, people to people. God our provider,
Hear our prayer.

Send your nourishment to our families. Draw members of each household to feast at the table of your divine love. Feed them

with your holy food and with living water, that every family, every person, every relationship would live according to your will. God our provider,
Hear our prayer.

We pray for those who are lost and wandering in the wilderness of this world, whose lives are filled with misery, homelessness, isolation, exploitation, and suffering. Send your help to bring them home into your divine presence. God our provider,
Hear our prayer.

We pray that you heal our sick, heal our relationships, heal our human spirits. *(Specific names are included here)*. God our provider,
Hear our prayer.

We remember those who have finished their earth's journey, and who feast at your eternal table of grace. As we remember and grieve, nourish us with your love. Give us the power of the resurrection and peace of heart, mind, and soul. God our provider,
Hear our prayer.

O God of love, we believe you hear and answer our prayers. We thank and praise you that, in our daily lives, the springs of your living water will be gushing up to eternal life, in and through Jesus Christ our Lord.
Amen.

Sending Dialogue

We are the people of God's realm.
By the Holy Spirit's guidance, we go forth as faithful witnesses of God's divine food and living water.

We are the disciples of our Lord Jesus, the Savior of the world.
By the Holy Spirit's guidance, we go forth to serve the hungry and the thirsty.

God's love has been poured into our hearts through the Holy Spirit.
By the Holy Spirit's guidance, we go forth to sow the seeds of God's love and grace.

Hymns

Come, Thou Fount Of Every Blessing
Come To Me, All Pilgrims Thirsty
Come, Ye Sinners, Poor And Needy
Great Is Thy Faithfulness
Guide Me Ever, Great Redeemer
I Heard The Voice Of Jesus Say
Jesus, Refuge Of The Weary
Lord Of Glory, You Have Bought Us
My Song Is Love Unknown
Rock Of Ages, Cleft For Me

Fourth Sunday in Lent

1 Samuel 16:1-13
Psalm 23
Ephesians 5:8-14
John 9:1-41

Call to Worship

We gather as children of light.
We gather to hear God's ways.

The Lord is our light and our salvation.
We believe in the Lord Jesus, light and savior of the world.

Glory be to God, now and forever.
Glory be to God, now and forever. Amen.

Collect / Prayer of the Day

God of life, through the crucified and risen Jesus, you offer eternal life. Open the eyes of our souls to see and receive your healing grace. Restore us and heal us of every blindness that keeps us from the life you intend for us. Make us witnesses of your light, in the name of Jesus Christ, our Lord. Amen.

Confession / Assurance of Forgiveness

If we walk in the light, as God is in the light, we have fellowship with one another.
God is holy. God is light. God is love.

Confessing our sin, we pray for the light of God to come into our lives.
{silent prayer for personal confession of sins}

God of light, our sin has blinded us to your will. We have sinned against you as the sheep of your pasture. We have wandered far from your word and your will. We have lost sight of your pathways to peace. We have blinded ourselves to those on our journey who are in need, those who are hungry, thirsty, lonely, losing their way. We have turned deaf ears to your calling to live as children of the light. Forgive us, O God. Restore sight to our blind eyes, hearing to our deaf ears, and your loving kindness to our hardened hearts, for the sake of Jesus Christ, our Savior and our Lord. Amen.

Give glory to God! For God gives you light, healing, love, and forgiveness. Once you were in darkness, but now you are in the light of the Lord. God forgives your sins, in the name of the Father, ✠ Son, and Holy Spirit.
Amen. Glory to God! Amen.

Prayers of the People / Prayers of Intercession
Healing God, throughout the ages you have provided leaders for your children. We give you thanks for church leaders in our day and ask that you sustain and strengthen them in their calling. Grant them your light and mercy to walk in your ways. God of light,
Hear our prayer.

We pray for the leaders and authorities of this nation, and all nations. Grant them wisdom, strength, and compassion. Give them fresh visions of justice. Give them the power, in all their decisions, to break down barriers of hate and greed. God of light,
Hear our prayer.

We pray for those who work for peace and justice in the darkness of our world. Shine your grace into our hearts and illuminate every corner of this world with your love. Let all your children open their eyes to see the abundance of your goodness. God of light,
Hear our prayer.

We pray that you heal the blindness of prejudice in the hearts of all your children. Bring the comfort of your grace to victims of prejudice, hate, and bullying. Open our eyes to see others as you see them. Wash away our sinful thoughts. With renewed vision, keep us from doing what is wrong in your eyes. God of light,
Hear our prayer.

We pray for those whose lives are torn asunder by warfare, terrorism, calamity, or natural disasters. Open the eyes of their souls to see that, in these troubles, you do not abandon them, and that you are present in healing and grace. God of light,
Hear our prayer.

We pray for the sick, the unemployed, the underemployed, the discouraged, those with disabilities or mental illness. We pray today for those whose needs are most known to our hearts in this moment. *(Specific names are included here)*. God of light,
Hear our prayer.

Give and send comfort and peace to the dying. Grant your heavenly light to those in grief. Enlighten all your children with the hope of everlasting life, that we all may sing your praises together, through all eternity. God of light,
Hear our prayer.

Guided by your Holy Spirit, we place into your care, O God of Light, all for whom we pray, trusting in your mercy, for the sake of your Son, Jesus Christ, our Lord.
Amen.

Sending Dialogue

Jesus called us to be "the light of the world."
We will be light-bearers where there is darkness in the world.

Let your light shine before others, so that God will be glorified.
The light of Christ will guide us in our daily living.

Thanks be to God for the divine light in our hearts!
Thanks be to God for the divine light in our hearts! Amen!

Hymns

Amazing Grace
Be Thou My Vision
Christ, The Life Of All The Living
God Is So Good
Let All Things Now Living
O Love, How Deep, How Broad, How High
Praise The One Who Breaks The Darkness
We Would Be Building
Wide Open Are Your Hands
What Wondrous Love Is This?

Fifth Sunday in Lent

Ezekiel 37:1-14
Psalm 130
Romans 8:6-11
John 11:1-45

Call to Worship

People of God, hope in the Lord.
We place our hope in God.

Be attentive to the Lord and receive steadfast love.
We will be attentive to the presence of God's love within us and among us.

Prepare your hearts. God will redeem you from all your iniquities.
We come to worship God with open minds and hearts.

Collect / Prayer of the Day

Eternal God, in every struggle, every sorrow, every death, you are the God of healing, peace, and life. You show up with life-giving power. Through this power, you call us to participate in your mission of freeing your daughters and sons from all that binds them. Strengthen and enable us to receive your life, and share your gifts in the world, through Jesus Christ, our Lord and Savior. Amen.

Confession / Assurance of Forgiveness

Out of the depths I cry to you, O Lord.
Lord, hear my voice.

Trusting that God is listening, bring your confession to God's forgiving heart.
{silent prayer for personal confession of sins}

Dear God, we come to you just as we are. We have heard your word many times, but we have allowed ourselves to ignore, even reject your will. Our spirit has sometimes become numb, even dead to your presence. We have failed to trust in your guidance. We confess that we have failed to be witnesses and instruments of your grace. We know that we stand in need of forgiveness. Restore us to newness of life, unbind us, and set us free, through our Savior, Jesus Christ. Amen.

There is good news for you. God is sending you the Holy Spirit, now. This is the Spirit of love. This is the Spirit of joy. This is the Spirit of peace. This is the Spirit of forgiveness. Know this: God is forgiving your sins and giving you new life in ✠ Jesus Christ our Lord.
Amen.

Prayers of the People / Prayers of Intercession

Eternal God, we pray that the church be a community that gives life to the world, extending your grace, light, and healing into the world. Send your church especially to hurting and injured places close to us, and places far away. God of life,
Hear us as we pray.

We bring our prayer for the nations of the world, that world leaders would promote human dignity and foster lasting peace. Bring the world out of death-places of war, terrorism, oppression, and violence. Unbind these places and people with new life, healing, and grace. God of life,
Hear us as we pray.

We pray for those paralyzed by fear, especially the fear of death and dying. We pray that the presence of your Son will give them new life and peace. God of life,
Hear us as we pray.

We pray for the poor and the hungry, the homeless and refugees, and all who are struggling to make ends meet. Bless them with your love, and let them know your love through people who are caring, compassionate, and called to serve. God of life,
Hear us as we pray.

We pray for those who grieve the deaths of loved ones, those are confounded by the pain of death, those who feel misunderstood, lonely, or neglected, those who struggle with various stages of grieving, especially anger and depression. We pray that you will give them deeper faith in Jesus and in his resurrection. God of life,
Hear us as we pray.

We pray for those who are sick, hospitalized, and homebound. Set them free, Lord, with your peace and healing. *(Specific names are included here)*. God of life,
Hear us as we pray.

We pray for deeper faith, that all who face death will clearly hear the voice of Christ Jesus calling us to eternal life. God of life,
Hear us as we pray.

Father in heaven, we thank you for hearing us this day. We know that you always hear us and are always near us. We thank you for the new life you are preparing for your people. We pray in the name of your Son, who lived and died, for the sake of the world.
Amen.

Sending Dialogue

Through the life, death, and resurrection of Jesus, remember that we are being saved.
We will always stand ready to receive God's new life.

Stand firm in the time of trial.
We will trust in God's ever-present, saving word.

Believe that Jesus is the Messiah, Son of God, the one who came into the world.
We will follow Jesus, the resurrection and the life, and we will serve in his name.

Hymns

Ask Ye What Great Thing I Know
Children Of The Heavenly Father
Draw Me Nearer
Forgive Our Sins As We Forgive
Guide Me Ever, Great Redeemer
Jesus, Refuge Of The Weary
Jesus, Thy Boundless Love To Me
My Hope Is Built On Nothing Less
My Life Flows On In Endless Song
Precious Lord, Take My Hand

Palm Sunday / Sunday of the Passion

Liturgy of the Palms
Matthew 21:1-11
Psalm 118:1-2, 19-29

Liturgy of the Passion
Isaiah 50:4-9a
Psalm 31:9-16
Philippians 2:5-11
Matthew 26:14–27:66 or Matthew 27:11-5

Call to Worship

Hosanna to the Son of David!
Blessed is he who comes in the name of the Lord! Hosanna to the Son of David!

We prepare now for the holiest of weeks.
We journey with praise on our lips. We remember the suffering and death of our Lord.

Blessed is he who comes in the name of the Lord!
Hosanna in the highest!

Collect / Prayer of the Day

Holy God, holy and immortal, as we enter into the week of the suffering and death of Jesus, we cling to the truth that you are with us in every place of suffering and death. Strengthen us to keep you at the center of our lives. Into your hands, O God, we commend ourselves and the world you love. In the name of the crucified Jesus, our Savior. Amen.

Confession / Assurance of Forgiveness

God calls us to a life of faithful holiness and obedience.
God calls us to follow the example of Jesus.

We confess our sins of unfaithfulness and disobedience.
{silent prayer for personal confession of sins}

Forgive us, O God, for our sins, our unfaithfulness, our disobedience. We confess we have not listened and heeded because of self-centeredness and weakness of spirit. We have sinned against you by our words, our actions, our thoughts. Forgive us, by the cross of Jesus Christ. Bring us back to a life of faithful discipleship where we neither doubt nor betray our Lord. In his name, we ask this. Amen.

Hear this word of God's love for you. God has heard your prayer, and God lovingly forgives your sins, in and through the crucified one, ✠ Jesus Christ, our Savior.
Amen.

Prayers of the People / Prayers of Intercession

God of our salvation, we pray in thanksgiving for the church in the world, and we pray that, in the church's struggles, you would keep us holy, united, unwavering, and compassionate in all things, and for all people. Nourish your church to bear good fruit. God of love,
Hear our prayer.

We pray that our hearts be fertile soil, so that your holy word within us remains a source of growth and nourishment. You have wonderfully made us, and yet we are sometime woefully hurting, suffering, anxious, and distressed. Embrace our hearts and souls, and heal us, to your glory. God of love,
Hear our prayer.

We pray for world leaders and governments, that decisions and laws be made according to your will. Fracture all hatefulness, oppression, injustice, and exploitation enacted against the innocent and vulnerable ones. Soften and heal the hardened hearts of those who would murder, do violence, and crucify your children. God of love,
Hear our prayer.

We pray for Christian communities suffering persecution, threats of violence, destruction of property. Protect and save them. God of love,
Hear our prayer.

We pray for families, and every kind of relationship, where there is tension, stress, even misery. Enter into their hearts and homes, O God, and bless their lives with redemption and reconciliation. God of love,
Hear our prayer.

We pray for the pains and sufferings of the sick. Grant them your healing Spirit. *(Specific names are included here).* God of love,
Hear our prayer.

With grief and tears, we remember those who have entered into death. Nurture the grieving ones and grant deep and abiding faith in the resurrection to eternal life. God of love,
Hear our prayer.

God of our salvation, we proclaim and embrace your eternal power over death and destruction. Hear our prayers and give all your children renewal, life, and grace. We ask this through Jesus Christ, our Lord.
Amen.

Sending Dialogue

As you go forth, know that the Lord God will be with you and help you.
My life, O God, is in your hands.

Seek the mind of Christ, who was humble, and exalted by God.
We will confess that Jesus Christ is Lord, to the glory of God the Father.

Jesus cried again with a loud voice and breathed his last.
Truly, this man was God's Son. Amen. Amen. Amen.

Hymns

Alas! And Did My Savior Bleed
All Glory, Laud, And Honor
Beneath The Cross Of Jesus
In The Cross Of Christ I Glory
Love Lifted Me
My Jesus, I Love Thee
O Sacred Head, Now Wounded
Ride On! Ride On In Majesty!
Were You There
When I Survey The Wondrous Cross

Maundy Thursday

Exodus 12:1-4 [5-10] 11-14
Psalm 116:1-2, 12-19
1 Corinthians 11:23-26
John 13:1-17, 31b-35

Call to Worship

This is the night we begin the solemn journey of the "Great Three Days" that changed the world and our lives. Followers of Jesus have been making this solemn journey since his first followers took it with him long ago.
We ask the Lord's blessings on this journey.

On this night, Jesus took a towel and a basin and washed the feet of the disciples. On this night, he told them to do the same for others, showing love for him and for one another, in humble service.
We hear the Lord's call for us to love and humbly serve one another.

On this night, Jesus celebrated the New Passover, breaking bread and sharing wine with his followers, inviting them to remember him by celebrating and continuing to partake of this meal.
We remember the abiding presence of the Lord Jesus.

This is the night when Christ Jesus, the Lamb of God, was betrayed, denied, and led away for trial and crucifixion.
We grieve and we rejoice in Jesus, who gave his life for us and for our salvation.

Collect / Prayer of the Day

God of love, on this holy night, we remember the sights and the sounds of the last Passover meal with the disciples. We remember the denials, the betrayals, the abandonments. We remember the humble washing of feet, and the call to do likewise. In accordance with the wishes of our Lord Jesus, we remember him. Tonight, we taste the forgiveness of sins. Tonight, we remember our commitment to love one another as your Son loved us. Tonight, we are blessed to remember your passionate love for us, in Jesus Christ, your Son, our Lord. Amen.

Confession / Assurance of Forgiveness

I give you a new commandment, that you love one another, just as I have loved you.
I give you a new commandment, that you love one another, just as I have loved you.

We now confess our sins, remembering all that we have said and done that has fallen short of God's glory.
{silent prayer for personal confession of sins}

God of grace, we confess that we have fallen short of your glory. You gave us ears to hear your word, but we do not listen. You gave us eyes to see our neighbor in need, but we avert our gaze. You gave us hands to serve, but we make stubborn fists to hurt others. You gave us each other, but we have disconnected and failed to love one another as your Son has loved us. Lord, our God, we are sorry for all our sins, for the wrongs we have done, for all the times we have failed to do good. Forgive us, Lord, and grant us peace. Restore us, now and always, that we might sit at your heavenly table with Jesus, our Lord and Savior. Amen.

Hear the truth of this night: divine love is revealed, not that we have loved God, but that God has loved us. By the power of the

cross and resurrection, God in ✠ Jesus Christ redeems us, forgives us, and restores us.
Amen.

Prayers of the People / Prayers of Intercession

Holy God, holy and immortal, we pray that your church would faithfully proclaim your message of good news and love to all the world. Loving God,
Hear our prayer.

We pray that, as disciples, we would fully embrace and live the commandment to love one another as our Savior has loved us. Loving God,
Hear our prayer.

We pray that you would make us into instruments of peace wherever we find conflict. Loving God,
Hear our prayer.

We pray for your protective hand upon the poor, the homeless, the oppressed, those who are being exploited, victims of violence and abuse. Send them the help they need, O Lord. Loving God,
Hear our prayer.

We pray for regions of the world torn by strife or violence. We pray for national and local leaders, that they would grow into humble, caring, foot-washing servants of those in their charge. Loving God,
Hear our prayer.

We pray for the sick and the suffering, that the life-giving presence of Jesus would bring them healing. *(Specific names are included here).* Loving God,
Hear our prayer.

Remembering those we love who have entered their eternal home, we pray for divine comfort and nourishment of soul, that God's resurrection-life would enter the hearts of all who grieve. Loving God,
Hear our prayer.

We bring you our prayers in the name of the one who died for us, Jesus Christ, our Savior.
Amen.

Sending Dialogue

Go forth in the strength of the Lord Jesus.
All praise, glory, and thanksgiving be to God.

Go forth doing good, and humbly serving others, in the name of the Lord Jesus.
All praise, glory, and thanksgiving be to God.

Go forth strengthened by the bread of life, Jesus himself.
All praise, glory, and thanksgiving be to God.

Hymns

Be Known To Us In Breaking Bread
Bread Of Life From Heaven
Go To Dark Gethsemane
Jesu, Jesu, Fill Us With Your Love
Just As I Am, Without One Plea
Lord Jesus Christ, We Humbly Pray
Lord, We Have Come At Your Own Invitation
Love Consecrates The Humblest Act
Where Charity And Love Prevail
You Satisfy The Hungry Heart

Good Friday

Isaiah 52:13–53:12
Psalm 22
Hebrews 10:16-25 or Hebrews 4:14-16; 5:7-9
John 18:1–19:42

Call to Worship
Be merciful to us, O God.
Show us your constant love.

We have done what is evil in your sight.
We have been sinful before you.

Create a pure heart within us, O God.
Put a new and faithful spirit within us.

Collect / Prayer of the Day
Almighty God, mindful of the events surrounding the death of your Son, we pray that you touch, cleanse, and purify our hearts. Pour your love into our hearts, and into the hearts of all your children. Direct us by your Holy Spirit to live lives of love and goodness. Grant us salvation, for the sake of Jesus Christ, our crucified Lord and Savior. Amen.

Confession / Assurance of Forgiveness
God so loved the world that he gave his only Son, so that everyone who believes in him may not perish, but may have eternal life.
Indeed, God did not send the Son into the world to condemn the world, but that the world might be saved through him.

We confess our sins, and the darkness of our hearts.
{silent prayer for personal confession of sins}

O Lord God, you have borne our griefs and carried our sorrows. You have been wounded for our transgressions, bruised for our iniquities. And we, like sheep, have gone astray. Again and again, our words and our actions have been wicked. We have called ourselves disciples, but we have abandoned you and the children you love. We have been slow to forgive and unwilling to reconcile. Have mercy on us, God of grace. Have mercy on us. Amen.

Christ Jesus offered himself, for all time, as a sacrifice for sins. Draw near to God with a true heart, in full assurance of redemption, the forgiveness of sins, and of eternal life in Christ. By his stripes, you are healed. By the sacrifice of his life, God forgives you your sins, through ✠ Jesus Christ our Lord.
Amen.

Prayers of the People / Prayers of Intercession

Saving God, remove from us all that is evil and place within us new and loyal hearts. Saving God,
Hear our prayer.

Open the hearts of your people to your abiding presence. Enliven us that we may know your truth, embrace your light, and reject all that is deceitful. Saving God,
Hear our prayer.

Comfort us when we weep bitterly out of sorrow because we have sinned against you. Grant us your mercy and abide with us. Draw us to yourself that we might place our lives in your hands. Saving God,
Hear our prayer.

Grant nations and leaders of every nation hearts of peace. Turn them away from hatefulness, oppression, and greed for power. Guide your children to unite together in the quest for peace. Draw all people to the life-giving cross. Saving God,
Hear our prayer.

Empower us to turn away from arrogance and selfishness, that we might increase our desire to serve others in your name, according to your will and purpose. Grant us your Spirit to discern the times to help others carry their crosses, and the times to rest with a quiet heart at the foot of our Savior's cross. Saving God,
Hear our prayer.

You are a God of love with compassion for all people. Hear us as we pray for those who are sick and suffering. *(Specific names are included here)*. Saving God,
Hear our prayer.

We remember today all our loved ones who have entered death. On this day of remembering that the Lord Jesus emptied himself, accepting death, even death on the cross, we look forward to his resurrection on the third day. In this remembering, O God, fill us with hope, light, and peace. Saving God,
Hear our prayer.

God, our God, we thank you for the gift of our Lord and Savior. As we bring our requests to you, we humbly bow before you and give you thanks. As we gather around the foot of the cross of your Son, accept our thanks and praise for all answered prayers. Most of all, we thank you for the life-giving sacrifice of Jesus our Lord, in whose name we pray.
Amen.

Sending Dialogue

We adore you, O Christ, and we bless you.
By your holy cross you have redeemed the world.

If we have died with him, we shall also live with him.
If we endure with him, we shall also reign with him.

We adore you, O Christ, and we bless you.
By your holy cross you have redeemed the world.

Hymns

Abide With Me
Ah, Holy Jesus
Alas! And Did My Savior Bleed
Beneath The Cross Of Jesus
In The Hour Of Trial
Jesus, Keep Me Near The Cross
O Sacred Head, Now Wounded
The Old Rugged Cross
Throned Upon The Awful Tree
Were You There?

Resurrection of the Lord / Easter Sunday

Acts 10:34-43 or Jeremiah 31:1-6
Psalm 118:1-2, 14-24
Colossians 3:1-4 or Acts 10:34-43
John 20:1-18 or Matthew 28:1-10

Call to Worship

Christ is risen! Alleluia!
Christ is risen indeed! Alleluia!

This is the day that the Lord has made! Alleluia!
We rejoice and are glad in it! Alleluia!

To God be the glory, forever and ever! Alleluia!
We worship and praise the risen Lord! Alleluia!

Worthy is Christ, the Lamb who was slain! Alleluia!
We worship and praise the risen Lord! Alleluia!

The Lord is my strength and my salvation! Alleluia!
We worship and praise the risen Lord! Alleluia!

Collect / Prayer of the Day

God of eternal life, by the life, death, and resurrection of your Son, you have conquered death. Today we celebrate that, in Christ, death does not have the last word. Your Word, your Son, your eternal life became the last word, the ultimate word. Grant us your Spirit to make us faithful witnesses of the resurrection, through Jesus Christ, our risen Lord. Amen.

Confession / Assurance of Forgiveness

In Christ, sin and death have lost their power over us!
We worship and praise the risen Lord! Alleluia! Alleluia! Alleluia!

Trusting in the power of the resurrection, we confess our sins.
{silent prayer for personal confession of sins}

God of the empty tomb, God of the resurrection, when we turn away from you and sin against others, we become locked in the darkest graves of sin and guilt. We become buried in darkness, separated from the life you gave us. Forgive us, O God, and free us. Pull us out of the tombs of sin. Raise us up to live our lives with your Son, whom you raised from death. Fill our lives with your forgiving grace and with the powerful light of the resurrection, though Jesus Christ, our risen Lord and Savior. Amen.

You are precious in God's sight! I declare: God frees you, lifts you up, and forgives your sins, in the name of ✠ Jesus Christ, our Risen Lord and Savior.
Amen.

Prayers of the People / Prayers of Intercession

God of eternal life, we praise and thank you for all the gifts that you lavish on your people through the victory of your Son. We thank you especially for the forgiveness of sins and eternal life. Make the people of your church to be living signs of the resurrection. Lord God of life,
Hear our prayer.

We pray for the nations of the world and every leader, that peace, justice, healing, and goodness might flourish in our day through the power of the resurrection. Lord God of life,
Hear our prayer.

We pray for those who cannot find a "Hallelujah" to sing in their lives today. Embrace them with your divine love. Give them your peace and comfort. Lord God of life,
Hear our prayer.

We pray that you would give all your children the wisdom, strength, and grace to embrace resurrection-faith and believe in your Son, our risen Lord Jesus. Lord God of life,
Hear our prayer.

We pray for your resurrection power to touch places in our world that are broken and torn apart. We pray especially for those most vulnerable, the weak, the chronically ill, the poor, the homeless, and refugees. Give your life to all who are afraid and anxious. Lord God of life,
Hear our prayer.

We pray for your healing to come upon all who are sick, in pain, or in distress. *(Specific names are included here)*. Lord God of life,
Hear our prayer.

Remembering those who have gone to their eternal home, we pray for all who grieve. Assure and comfort them with the hope, the peace, and the joy of the resurrection. Lord God of life,
Hear our prayer.

Receive these prayers, O God of the resurrection, and all the prayers of your beloved children, through Jesus Christ our Lord and Savior.
Amen.

Sending Dialogue

You have been raised with Christ. Alleluia!
We go now into the world as resurrection witnesses. Alleluia!

Set your minds on things that are above.
We will set our minds on Christ Jesus and his resurrection. We will live our daily lives in him!

Christ is risen! Alleluia!
Christ is risen indeed! Alleluia!

Hymns

Alleluia, Alleluia, Give Thanks
At The Lamb's High Feast We Sing
Come, Ye Faithful, Raise The Strain
Christ The Lord Is Risen Today!
Day Of Arising
Jesus Christ Is Risen Today
Now All The Vault Of Heaven Resounds
The Day Of Resurrection
That Easter Day With Joy Was Bright
Thine Is The Glory

Second Sunday of Easter

Acts 2:14a, 22-32
Psalm 16
1 Peter 1:3-9
John 20:19-31

Call to Worship
Christ is risen! Alleluia!
Christ is risen indeed! Alleluia!

To God be the glory, forever and ever!
We worship and praise the Risen Lord!

Jesus stands among us, offering us peace.
The risen Lord is here in our midst. Alleluia!

Collect / Prayer of the Day
My Lord and my God, although we have not seen you, we believe in you and in the resurrection to eternal life. We praise and thank you that, by your power and love, we are receiving the outcome of our faith, the salvation of our souls. Fortify our souls as we rejoice in the indescribable and glorious joy of the resurrection, through Jesus Christ, our risen Lord. Amen.

Confession / Assurance of Forgiveness
Protect me, O God, for in you I take refuge.
You are my Lord. Apart from you I have no good.

Our sorrows have been multiplied by our sin, and so, before God and one another, we confess our sins.
{silent prayer for personal confession of sins}

God of grace, we praise you with our voices, we sing "alleluia," we proclaim your good news. But we confess, there are times when, by the way we live our lives, we show disbelief. We avoid your community of faith. We cling to our possessions with our hearts fixed on them. We overlook injustice. We ignore the poor and those in need. We fail to take proper care of the lives of others, even our own lives. Forgive us, Lord. Restore us to your heart, and make us a new creation, through Jesus Christ our Lord. Amen.

Blessed are you who have not seen and yet have come to believe. Receive the Holy Spirit. Receive the peace of Jesus Christ. Receive God's forgiveness of your sins, through ✠ Jesus Christ our Lord.
Amen.

Prayers of the People / Prayers of Intercession
God of new life, increase the faith of your church, to faithfully witness to your love, your forgiveness, your resurrection. Hear us, Lord of glory.
Lord, hear our prayer.

We pray that, when waves of conflict, hardship, and doubt flood the lives of your children, your Son would enter in with his heart of peace. Hear us, Lord of glory.
Lord, hear our prayer.

Reveal the power of your resurrection to the leaders of every nation, especially those who are far outside your will. Raise them up from lives of violence, destruction, cruelty, abuse, injustice, oppression, and greed. Give new life to our world, that your peace, love, and compassion would abound everywhere. Hear us, Lord of glory.
Lord, hear our prayer.

We pray for those who have been blinded to signs of your glory in their lives. Shatter their darkness with your gentle love and your invitation to be at peace. Hear us, Lord of glory.
Lord, hear our prayer.

We pray for those who ache with loneliness, those who suffer with hunger, confusion, anxiety, despair. Send them your holy compassion. Send them angels, ministers, and caretakers to bring them your healing and peace. Hear us, Lord of glory.
Lord, hear our prayer.

We pray for those who are afflicted with illness. Grant them your healing presence, O God. *(Specific names are included here).* Hear us, Lord of glory.
Lord, hear our prayer.

We pray for those who are weighed down by grief. Give them deep, abiding resurrection-joy in your victory over sin, death, and every evil. Hear us, Lord of glory.
Lord, hear our prayer.

Almighty God, we bring our prayers to you in faith. Hear us, we pray, and come to us in your love and your peace, through Christ our Lord.
Amen.

Sending Dialogue

Jesus has come to us offering peace.
As we receive his peace, we will carry it into our homes, our relationships, the whole world.

We have prayed for the hungry and those in need.
We will be instruments of God's goodness and generosity.

Christ is risen! Alleluia!
Christ is risen indeed! Alleluia!

Hymns

Alleluia! Jesus Is Risen
Blessing And Honor
Christ Is Alive! Let Christians Sing
Christ Is Risen! Alleluia!
How Great Thou Art
I'm So Glad Jesus Lifted Me
Now The Green Blade Rises
Oh, Sing To The Lord
O Zion, Haste
The Strife Is O'er, The Battle Done

Third Sunday of Easter

Acts 2:14a, 36-41
Psalm 116:1-4, 12-19
1 Peter 1:17-23
Luke 24:13-35

Call to Worship
We gather in the presence of God and in the presence of God's people.
Our faith and our hope rest in God.

I will lift up the cup of salvation.
I will call on the name of the LORD.

God shows us the path of life.
In God's presence, there is fullness of joy. Alleluia!

Collect / Prayer of the Day
Lord God, we rejoice in the resurrection of Jesus, your Son our Lord. We long to recognize him, and be present with him. As we travel on our journey of life, guide us on the right paths, always walking with your Son. Make our hearts burn within us, and, finally, bring us to the fullness of your presence, the eternal feast, life forever and forever. Amen.

Confession / Assurance of Forgiveness
We call on the name of the Lord.
O Lord, I pray, save my life!

We are invited to repent in the name of Jesus Christ so that our sins may be forgiven.
{silent prayer for personal confession of sins}

Good and gracious God, you call us to be your disciples in a lonely, strife-filled, hungry generation. We have turned from your ways. We have rejected the gospel. We have not obeyed your good and holy will. Forgive us, O God of our redemption. Embrace us with your love. Renew us through the life, death, and resurrection of our Lord and Savior. Amen.

By your confession, your souls are purified by your obedience to the truth. God is enriching you with genuine, deep love from your heart. You have been born anew, not by perishable things like silver or gold, but by the precious blood of Christ. In him, ✠ Jesus Christ, our Lord, God forgives your sins.
Amen.

Prayers of the People / Prayers of Intercession

Gracious God, we give you thanks for the victory of Christ Jesus. Give us eyes to see the signs of his victory in our daily lives, and to recognize his presence with us. Give us hearts filled with genuine love. God of life,
Hear our prayer.

Remembering our baptism every day, grant us your Holy Spirit to help us travel with Jesus on our daily journey. God of life,
Hear our prayer.

We pray for your children who are wandering aimlessly, for those searching for the imperishable love you offer, for those searching for meaning in their lives, for those who struggle with rejection and loneliness. Send them your Holy Spirit, according to their needs. God of life,
Hear our prayer.

We pray that the leaders of the nations of the world would act justly and bring peace to the people. Help them to find ways to lift up the value and dignity of each person. God of life,
Hear our prayer.

We pray for all who are afflicted, for the physically and spiritually hungry, for those trapped in the clutches of addiction. Welcome them to your table, O God, and feed them with your divine blessings. God of life,
Hear our prayer.

We pray for your healing to rest upon all who are sick, in pain, or in distress. *(Specific names are included here)*. God of life,
Hear our prayer.

We give thanks for all the faithful witnesses who have gone before us and are now in heaven. In our grieving, immerse us in the light and glory of the resurrection. God of life,
Hear our prayer.

We thank you, Lord, that you have inclined your ear to us. You have heard our voices and our supplications. We will continue to call on you as long as we live. Anoint our hearts that they always burn within us in the presence of your love, your glory, and your new life, through Jesus Christ our Lord.
Amen.

Sending Dialogue

God of the resurrection, I am your companion.
I will walk in your presence all my days.

God of the resurrection, I am your servant.
I will serve others in your name.

God of the resurrection, I am your child.
I will love as you have loved me.

Hymns

Borning Cry
Day Of Arising
I Bind Unto Myself Today
I Know That My Redeemer Lives!
Lord Of All Hopefulness
O Sons And Daughters, Let Us Sing
Take My Life, That I May Be
That Easter Day With Joy Was Bright
We Are Baptized In Christ Jesus
Ye Servants Of God

Fourth Sunday of Easter

Acts 2:42-47
Psalm 23
1 Peter 2:19-25
John 10:1-10

Call to Worship
As God's people, we gather for worship, receiving God's love, grace, mercy, peace, and forgiveness.
Jesus is our Shepherd. We follow him.

In every valley, God's goodness and mercy are with us.
Jesus is our Shepherd. We follow him.

God promises that, in Christ, our dwelling place is always in the presence of God.
Jesus is our Shepherd. We follow him.

Jesus gave his life for his sheep.
To Jesus our Shepherd be all glory, honor, worship, and praise. Amen! Alleluia! Amen!

Collect / Prayer of the Day
God, our Great Shepherd, we rejoice today in the gifts of abundant life and salvation in your Son. We thank you for divine protection, nourishment, peace, and for all your gifts. Keep us from fear and from going astray and help us to immerse our lives in your love. Inspire us by your Holy Spirit to focus our lives on Jesus as our example for living. Guide us to follow in his steps all the days of our lives. In Jesus' name we pray. Amen.

Confession / Assurance of Forgiveness

Jesus, our Savior and Shepherd, came into our world to redeem us.

Jesus himself bore our sins in his body on the cross, so that, free from sins, we might live for righteousness.

Preparing to receive divine mercy and love, we confess our sins.
{silent prayer for personal confession of sins}

Almighty God, we confess that we have wandered from the path of righteousness. We have refused your goodness and mercy. We have not always followed your Son, our true and only shepherd. For his sake, have mercy on us and forgive us. Renew us and lead us, that we may dwell in your house forever. Amen.

Jesus said: "I am the good shepherd. The good shepherd lays down his life for the sheep... I am the good shepherd. I know my own and my own know me." Through his life, death, and resurrection, I assure you that God forgives your sins, through the cross and resurrection of ✠ Jesus Christ, our Good Shepherd, our Lord, our Savior.
Amen. Thanks be to God! Amen.

Prayers of the People / Prayers of Intercession

God our loving God, in your infinite wisdom and loving care, guide all the people of the world to recognize and follow your Son. God our shepherd,
Hear our prayer.

Through this worship, grant us spiritual hearing to recognize your voice more clearly. Gently call all your children by name, remind us of your eternal love, and grant us endurance for every suffering. God our shepherd,
Hear our prayer.

Inspire the leaders of every nation to walk in your ways, so that all people are free to receive the abundant life you offer and promise. Turn every leader away from injustice, oppression, and everything that is not aligned with your will. God our shepherd,
Hear our prayer.

We pray that you provide strength to those who work in dangerous and difficult places, laboring to provide for the well-being and safety of your flock. God our shepherd,
Hear our prayer.

We pray for your presence with those who are walking through dark valleys, overshadowed by anxiety and fear, overwhelmed with pain and suffering. Send your help and nourishment to the hungry, the thirsty, the poor, the unemployed, the under-employed. Direct your church to be servants of those in need. God our shepherd,
Hear our prayer.

Strengthen, anoint, and bless all in need of healing. *(Specific names are included here)*. God our shepherd,
Hear our prayer.

We give thanks for all believers who heard and followed your voice in this life and who now dwell with you forever. Walk with those who grieve and embrace them with your love. God our shepherd,
Hear our prayer.

Receive our prayers, O God, for the sake of your Son, our Good Shepherd, Jesus Christ, our Lord.
Amen.

Sending Dialogue

Jesus, great shepherd of the sheep, will provide for all we need.
We will rest in God, and drink from divine, peaceful waters.

Jesus, our Good Shepherd, will restore us and nourish us.
We will travel in the ways of doing what is right.

God anoints us and gives us overflowing love every day.
We will receive and we will bring God's goodness and mercy to others.

Hymns

Be Not Afraid
Blessed Assurance
Blessing And Honor
Have No Fear, Little Flock
He Leadeth Me
I Heard The Voice Of Jesus Say
I Know My Redeemer Lives!
Jesus, Shepherd Of Our Souls
Savior, Like A Shepherd Lead Us
The King Of Love My Shepherd Is

Fifth Sunday of Easter

Acts 7:55-60
Psalm 31:1-5, 15-16
1 Peter 2:2-10
John 14:1-14

Call to Worship
As God's people, we gather for worship.
We gather to receive God's love, grace, mercy, peace, and forgiveness.

God is about to do new things.
We seek new life in Jesus Christ.

Come to him, a living stone, and let yourselves be built into a spiritual house.
We are a chosen people, a royal priesthood, a holy nation. We are God's own people.

Collect / Prayer of the Day
O Lord, faithful God, you have made your Son our cornerstone, chosen and precious. You have created us as living stones, to make us into a spiritual house, a holy priesthood. Increase our faith, give us a foretaste of eternal life, unite us in the fellowship of believers, through Jesus Christ, our way, our truth, our life. Amen.

Confession / Assurance of Forgiveness
Take refuge in the Lord.
God is our rock and our fortress.

As followers of Jesus, we ask God for forgiveness.
{silent prayer for personal confession of sins}

Loving and almighty God, we confess that we have failed, even refused, to follow your Son. We have wandered and become lost by turning away from you. Forgive us by your grace. Fill us with your peace. Give us confidence to follow your Son, Jesus Christ, our Lord and Savior. Amen.

Hear the good news: Christ Jesus died and rose again for the sake of the world, overthrowing the powers of sin and death. We are set free to follow Christ, no longer enslaved by the powers of sin and darkness. In ✠ Jesus Christ, God forgives your sins and redeems you. Believe this good news of the gospel!
We believe! Thanks be to God! Amen!

Prayers of the People / Prayers of Intercession

Faithful God, all your words and works are trustworthy. Deliver and preserve all your children through the life, death, and resurrection of your Son. O Lord, our faithful God,
Hear our prayer.

Grant your church the grace to channel your love into the lives of all people. Kindle in us the willingness to bring your word into the world, by deeds of kindness and words of hope and truth. O Lord, our faithful God,
Hear our prayer.

Guide leaders of the nations with your divine strength and wisdom, that all communities may be safe places for children, adults, seniors, infants, and youth. O Lord, our faithful God,
Hear our prayer.

Send your divine care to those who are hungry, exiled, threatened by terror and violence, victims of war, oppressed, and injured. Grant them peace, justice, compassion, and healing. O Lord, our faithful God,
Hear our prayer.

Be ever present with those who are persecuted for their faith. Protect them and deliver them from the hands of those who would do them harm. Let your face shine upon them and save them by your steadfast love. O Lord, our faithful God,
Hear our prayer.

Hear our prayer for all who are sick. Calm the hearts of all who are troubled in any way. *(Specific names are included here)*. O Lord, our faithful God,
Hear our prayer.

Bless the tears of all who grieve. Give assurance and hope in the resurrection to life eternal. O Lord, our faithful God,
Hear our prayer.

God of eternal life, we trust you. Hear our prayers and let your mercy be upon us. We ask in the name of Jesus Christ our Lord.
Amen.

Sending Dialogue
As you go forth, continue to grow into salvation.
We will proclaim, in words and actions, the mighty acts of God.

Do not grow weary of doing what is right.
We will live every day as disciples of Jesus Christ!

We go with the grace of the Lord, Jesus Christ.
We will serve others where God calls us to serve.

Hymns

All Are Welcome
Blest Be The Tie That Binds
Built On A Rock
Faith Of Our Fathers
Lord, Whose Love In Humble Service
O Christ, Your Heart, Compassionate
Our Father, By Whose Name
When Morning Gilds The Skies
You Are The Way
You That Know The Lord Is Gracious

Sixth Sunday of Easter

Acts 17:22-31
Psalm 66:8-20
1 Peter 3:13-22
John 14:15-21

Call to Worship
Praise God and let the sound of God's praise be heard.
Praise to the Lord of heaven and earth.

We gather in the presence of the God who made the world and everything in it.
In Christ, we live and move and have our being.

We are God's offspring.
God's Spirit abides with us and is within us.

Collect / Prayer of the Day
God, our redeemer, you have sent your Son into the world and given him to us, calling us to be his disciples. He promised to send us an advocate, a helper, a counselor, a comforter, your Holy Spirit. Empower us to rely on your Spirit for daily life in Christ. Strengthen us to keep your commandments, always living with your love in our hearts. In the name of Jesus, we pray. Amen.

Confession / Assurance of Forgiveness
If you love me, you will keep my commandments.
It is God's will that all people everywhere repent.

Repentance is turning ourselves around, back to God. We confess our sins.
{silent prayer for personal confession of sins}

God, our redeemer, your word is strength, and your ways are life. We confess that we have not always listened to your word. We have not always followed your ways. We have become weakened by our sin. We have lived in the shadow of death, not life. We have been unholy in our actions, apathetic in our discipleship, sinful in thought, word, and deed. Forgive us, O God. Lead us back to you, walking in the steps of Jesus. Forgive us in his name. Amen.

Jesus said: "Those who have my commandments and keep them are those who love me." As your request for forgiveness is a sign of love within you, know this: God loves you and forgives you, through the cross and resurrection of ✠ Jesus Christ, our Lord and Savior.
Amen.

Prayers of the People / Prayers of Intercession

Eternal God, we give you thanks for this day of worship. Guide us by your Holy Spirit when life is troubled and when life is calm. Keep us always strong to do your will. Holy God,
Hear our prayer.

Be present with the church on earth, that the church would faithfully serve all who hunger for your divine presence. Through the work of the church, gather in, with gentleness and reverence, those who are spiritual orphans. Embrace them with the love of your heart. Holy God,
Hear our prayer.

Send your Spirit to the leaders of the nations, that divisions would become transformed into ways of cooperation for the well-being of all people. Bring peace to the nations of the world. Holy God,
Hear our prayer.

Preserve the hungry from famine, rescue the oppressed from pain and death, deliver our world from destruction. Holy God,
Hear our prayer.

Strengthen all the ministries of this community of faith, that your divine care and compassion might be made known through us. Holy God,
Hear our prayer.

We lift up to you those whose lives are burdened with sickness, disease, and afflictions of any kind. *(Specific names are included here)*. Holy God,
Hear our prayer.

We thank you for all the saints who have been examples of worshiping and serving your reign. Comfort the grieving and give them deep and abiding hope in the resurrection. Holy God,
Hear our prayer.

Eternal God, heed the words of our prayers, those spoken and those unspoken, and give us your steadfast love, in the name and Spirit of Jesus Christ our Lord.
Amen.

Sending Dialogue

Jesus says: "Because I live, you also will live."
Because Jesus lives, we will live in him.

Because Jesus forgives and serves,
We will forgive and serve.

Because Jesus heals and loves,
We will heal and love.

Hymns

Awake, My Heart, With Gladness
Come, Ye Faithful, Raise The Strain
How Firm A Foundation
Lord, Speak To Us, That We May Speak
Love Divine, All Loves Excelling
O Love That Will Not Let Me Go
Praise To The Lord, The Almighty
Spirit Of Gentleness
The Church's One Foundation
What Wondrous Love Is This?

Ascension of the Lord

These readings may also be used on the Seventh Sunday of Easter.

Acts 1:1-11
Psalm 47 or Psalm 93
Ephesians 1:15-23
Luke 24:44-53

Call to Worship
Jesus ascended and sits at the right hand of God.
Sing praise to God, sing praise. Our God reigns over all the earth.

We gather as God's people, to worship and honor God.
Sing praise to God, sing praise. Our God reigns over all the earth.

We proclaim that, through the crucified and risen Lord Jesus, God loves, comforts, and speaks to us.
Sing praise to God, sing praise. Our God reigns over all the earth.

Collect / Prayer of the Day
God of the universe, through the life, suffering, death, resurrection, and ascension of our Lord Jesus, you have commissioned us to carry on his work in the world. Guide your church, which you have fashioned to be the Body of Christ on earth, to bring your love, forgiveness, mercy, and compassion to all people. We pray in the name of Jesus, our Lord. Amen.

Confession / Assurance of Forgiveness

Thus it is written, that the Messiah is to suffer and to rise from the dead on the third day, and that repentance and forgiveness of sins is to be proclaimed in his name to all nations.
Thanks be to God for the forgiveness of sins.

We now confess our sins with honesty of heart.
{silent prayer for personal confession of sins}

God of glory, we confess that, while we know and believe the story of Jesus, we sometimes do not allow our faith to make a difference in our lives. We fail to value each other as Jesus values everyone. We fail to serve. We fail to witness. We fail to love as he loved us. We do harm to others and ourselves. Forgive us, O God. Enhance our discipleship, give us grace to grow, and inspire us to serve in the name of our risen and ascended Savior. Amen.

God, creator of the world, raised Jesus from the dead, who is seated at God's right hand in the heavenly places. You are called to participate in creating a reign of goodness and love. With a heart of repentance, you are gifted for the task, and God forgives you, in ✠ Jesus Christ our Lord.
Amen. Thanks be to God! Amen.

Prayers of the People / Prayers of Intercession

Almighty God, we pray for the church, that we all may be one in Christ, that believers would be faithful servants and give glory to you. Lord, in your mercy,
Hear our prayer.

We pray for all who govern the nations of the world, that you would create for them paths to peace and justice for all people. Lord, in your mercy,
Hear our prayer.

We pray that your grace and care be upon the poor and oppressed, prisoners and captives, exiles and the lost, and for all who minister and care for them. Lord, in your mercy,
Hear our prayer.

We pray for places affected by storms, floods, and wildfires. Give hope to suffering families. Grant safety to those who work to rescue those in trouble and distress. Grant strength and wisdom to those working to rebuild their lives. Lord, in your mercy,
Hear our prayer.

We pray for all children, that homes, schools, and churches be safe places for them. Protect them from every evil and harm. Keep them in your loving care. Lord, in your mercy,
Hear our prayer.

We pray for all who are sick, in pain, or in distress. *(Specific names are included here)*. Lord, in your mercy,
Hear our prayer.

We remember with affection our loved ones who have gone to their eternal place in heaven. Comfort those who grieve with assurance of the resurrection. Lord, in your mercy,
Hear our prayer.

Hear and answer our prayers, holy God, through Jesus Christ, our Lord.
Amen.

Sending Dialogue

Honor, glory, and praise to the one who sits on the throne!
Alleluia! Alleluia! Alleluia!

"Be my witnesses … to the ends of the earth," says the Lord.
We go into the world as witnesses of God's love.

The Holy Spirit will guide us and inspire us.
"Your word is a lamp to my feet and a light to my path."

Hymns

A Hymn of Glory Let Us Sing!
Beautiful Savior
Borning Cry
Crown Him With Many Crowns
Here I Am, Lord
Holy, Holy, Holy, Lord God Almighty!
O Savior, Precious Savior
On Eagle's Wings
Renew Thy Church, Her Ministries Restore
Shine, Jesus, Shine

Seventh Sunday of Easter

Acts 1:6-14
Psalm 68:1-10, 32-35
1 Peter 4:12-14; 5:6-11
John 17:1-11

Call to Worship
Let us be joyful and praise God.
We will sing to God, and praise God's name.

Listen! For God speaks to us in a mighty voice.
Holy and awesome is God's power and strength.

God provides for the needs of all people.
Blessed be God! Praise God's name!

Collect / Prayer of the Day
God of glory, you sent your Son to bring eternal life to the people of the world. He made your name, your heart, and your presence known. Draw us today to receive him and accept his love for us. By your Holy Spirit, strengthen us to cast all our anxiety into the sea of your grace. Transform us and keep us alert to your divine presence in our lives. To Christ be all glory forever and ever. Amen.

Confession / Assurance of Forgiveness
Humble yourselves under the mighty hand of God.
God will exalt us, and lift us up, in due time.

And now, we confess our sins before the God of our salvation.
{silent prayer for personal confession of sins}

God of steadfast love, we turn to you for your divine protection. We have failed to resist temptations. We have not been steadfast in our faith. We have ignored our brothers and sisters who undergo suffering. We have been self-centered and uncaring. Forgive us, remove selfishness from our hearts, teach us your will, and renew us in faith and courage to follow your Son, Jesus Christ, our Lord. Amen.

People of God, you are blessed, because the Spirit of Glory, the very Spirit of God, is resting upon you. Through the Holy Spirit, God restores, supports, strengthens, places you on a firm foundation, and forgives your sins for the sake of ✠ Jesus Christ. To God be the glory and power forever and ever.
Amen.

Prayers of the People / Prayers of Intercession

Good and gracious God, we celebrate again today that Jesus our Lord, called the church to receive his mission. As the hour of his passion drew near, he prayed for us. Through his prayer, keep the church in unity, always one with you. Holy Father,
Hear our prayer.

Bring healing to the brokenness of the world. Give light to those who struggle with inner darkness. Shelter, protect, and send help to families that are in distress, churches that are divided, victims of violence, people oppressed by governments, refugees trying to escape war, those who are persecuted, the hungry, and those afflicted with disasters. Holy Father,
Hear our prayer.

In your goodness, O God, provide for those in need physically, mentally, emotionally, and spiritually. Grant them your grace, love, and protection through the ministries of the church, through prayer and service. Holy Father,
Hear our prayer.

We pray that our homes be filled with your presence and your love. Send your Spirit to make our homes places of faithfulness, integrity, and generosity. Holy Father,
Hear our prayer.

Send your Spirit to set free those who are in bondage to fear, despair, anxiety, or hatred. Give them new life. Give them your love. Holy Father,
Hear our prayer.

Provide healing and comfort to all who are battling sickness of every kind. *(Specific names are included here).* Holy Father,
Hear our prayer.

We pray for all who grieve. Fill them, and all of us, with the power of your glorious resurrection. Holy Father,
Hear our prayer.

As the Lord Jesus summons us to pray, we ask, O God, that you lovingly hear our prayers and embrace us and all people. In his holy, precious name we pray.
Amen.

Sending Dialogue

This is eternal life, that we know the only true God, in Jesus Christ.
We will keep God's word in our daily living.

Jesus has spoken God's word to us and to the world.
We will receive the holy word of God and daily put it into practice.

Jesus finished his work on earth, giving perfect glory to God.
We will be witnesses to the world that God sent Jesus for our salvation.

Hymns

Alleluia! Sing To Jesus
Christ Is Alive! Let Christians Sing
Eternal God, Whose Power Upholds
God Himself Is Present
How Firm A Foundation
Joyful, Joyful We Adore Thee
Lord, Take My Hand And Lead Me
Lord, You Give The Great Commission
My Faith Looks Up To Thee
Rise Up, O Saints Of God!

Day of Pentecost

Acts 2:1-21 or Numbers 11:24-30
Psalm 104:24-34, 35b
1 Corinthians 12:3b-13 or Acts 2:1-21
John 20:19-23 or John 7:37-39

Call to Worship

The Day of Pentecost is here!
The Holy Spirit comes upon us, inflame our hearts, and remain with us always.

May the flames of faith dance in our hearts.
The Spirit of peace brings calm to every fearful and anxious heart.

May our babbling speech become good news for the world.
God's Spirit transforms us into compassionate, loving, joyful disciples.

Collect / Prayer of the Day

Eternal God, we praise and thank you for the gift of the Holy Spirit, the tongues of fire, the mighty wind, and your eternal, divine presence. Strengthen your church on this Day of Pentecost, that the fire of your love will blaze within us and that your divine energy will surge in the whole world. Empower us, and all the world to speak your language of forgiveness, compassion, and sacrificial love, through Jesus Christ our Lord, in whom we pray. Amen.

Confession / Assurance of Forgiveness

Jesus promised he would not abandon us. He would send the Spirit of truth to us, to be with us forever.

God's Holy Spirit is always with us, leading us, guiding us, inspiring us, calling us, comforting us.

As we pray that God's Spirit comes to us, bringing grace, hope, and forgiveness, we confess our sins to God in the silence of our hearts.
{silent prayer for personal confession of sins}

Merciful God, we confess that we all have sinned. We confess our sins as a church. We have not loved one another as Christ has loved us. We have not comforted one another as Christ comforts us. We have not forgiven one another as we have been forgiven. We have not given ourselves in service as Christ gave himself for us. In your mercy, forgive us and embrace us with your love. Open our hearts to receive your Spirit. Strengthen us to live according to your will as faithful disciples of your Son, Jesus Christ, our Lord and Savior, in whose name we pray. Amen.

God strengthens us, heals our brokenness, and looks upon us with mercy. God forgives us and restores us to new life, in the name of the Father, ✠ Son, and Holy Spirit.
Amen.

Prayers of the People / Prayers of Intercession

We pray that the Holy Spirit inspire and guide all who confess Jesus as Lord, that we would live in unity as faithful disciples, servants, and ministers of the gospel. Come, Holy Spirit,
Hear our prayer.

We pray that the Holy Spirit bring peace to all who are troubled, comfort to the lonely, reconciliation to those who are separated, light to those in darkness, and love to all God's children. Come, Holy Spirit,
Hear our prayer.

We pray that the Holy Spirit move leaders and nations to work for true peace and justice, and put away all violence, greed, and oppression. Come, Holy Spirit,
Hear our prayer.

We pray that the Holy Spirit bring relief to the poor, release to those bound by sin, addiction, and transgressions against the will of God. Come, Holy Spirit,
Hear our prayer.

We pray that the Holy Spirit inspire and excite young and old to use their creative talents and gifts for building up the body of Christ in this place and time. Come, Holy Spirit,
Hear our prayer.

We pray that the Holy Spirit bring healing to those who are sick, compassion to those in distress of any kind. *(Specific names are included here)*. Come, Holy Spirit,
Hear our prayer.

We pray that the Holy Spirit comfort all who grieve, bestowing the gift of peace and the promise of everlasting life to surround and uphold them. Come, Holy Spirit,
Hear our prayer.

Loving God, you are near to us when we cry out to you. Into your embrace we commend all for whom we pray, through Christ Jesus and by the power of your Spirit.
Amen.

Sending Dialogue

The Holy Spirit pours grace into our lives.
By the Spirit's power, we will speak God's language of love.

The Holy Spirit will dispel our darkness.
By the Spirit's power, we will live in God's light.

The Holy Spirit calls us to be disciples of Jesus.
By the Spirit's power, we will tell the good news.

Hymns

Breathe On Me, Breath Of God
Come, Gracious Spirit, Heavenly Dove
Holy Spirit, Ever Dwelling
Holy Spirit, Truth Divine
O Breath Of Life
O Holy Spirit, Root Of Life
O Spirit Of The Living God
Spirit Blowing Through Creation
Spirit Of God, Descend Upon My Heart
Spirit Of The Living God

Trinity Sunday

Genesis 1:1--2:4a
Psalm 8
2 Corinthians 13:11-13
Matthew 28:16-20

Call to Worship

We gather in the name of the Father, creator of the world.
We praise and worship God, the Father.

We gather in the name of Jesus, the Son, Savior of the world.
We praise and worship God, the Son.

We gather in the name of the Spirit, present in our lives, always blessing us with holiness.
We praise and worship God, the Holy Spirit.

Collect / Prayer of the Day

Eternal God — Father, Son, and Holy Spirit — you have made yourself known to the children of your creation in countless ways over the centuries. You have made yourself known in your glorious creation. You made yourself known to Moses, the prophets, and your chosen people. In the fullness of time, you made yourself known by giving Jesus to us. You appeared on the mountain of the Transfiguration and your presence was known in the miracles and parables, most clearly in the suffering, death, and resurrection of Jesus. You made yourself known on Pentecost, sending the Holy Spirit in wind, fire, and various tongues. We thank you that you continued to make yourself known in the church through the centuries, and in our day. Open our minds and hearts to know you always as Father, Son, and Holy Spirit. Amen.

Confession / Assurance of Forgiveness

Blessed be the Holy Trinity, one God, whose name is majestic in all the earth.
God rescues us and heals us in every trouble.

Before God, we confess our sins.
{silent prayer for personal confession of sins}

Almighty God, we confess that we have misused your gift of creation. We have been ungrateful and been poor stewards of creation. We have denied, even betrayed our Lord Jesus. We have neglected to abide by his teachings. We have resisted the leading and guidance of the Holy Spirit. Forgive us, O God. Grant us your mercy. Wash away the sin within us. Cleanse, heal, and renew us in your love. By your grace, lead us to everlasting life. Amen.

Hear good news! God forgives you and restores you to new life! In this forgiveness, God strengthens you, heals your brokenness, and gives you mercy, peace, and hope. In thanksgiving, receive God's forgiveness, in the name of the Father, ✠ Son, and Holy Spirit.
Amen.

Prayers of the People / Prayers of Intercession

Creator God, we give you thanks for the beautiful and bountiful world. We pray that your creation be a sign to all people of your power, might, and love. Inspire us to work for the well-being of the earth and all its creatures. Holy God,
Hear our prayer.

As your holy people, grant unity to the church, unite us as your created ones, disciples of Jesus, stirred up and inspired by your Spirit. Holy God,
Hear our prayer.

Bring healing to the world, the earth, the nations, and all the people who dwell therein. We give you thanks for those whose vocation is to bring healing to the world. Holy God,
Hear our prayer.

Send your Spirit to those filled with doubt. Gently embrace them with your loving compassion, your holy understanding, and your divine truth. Holy God,
Hear our prayer.

Grant and send help and relief to those in need, and all who experience troubles, difficulties, and frustrations of life. Especially we ask you to send protection to the oppressed, the abused, the bullied, the victimized. Holy God,
Hear our prayer.

Send divine healing to those who are sick, troubled, distressed, discouraged, and weakened in health. *(Specific names are included here)*. Holy God,
Hear our prayer.

Comfort and send your divine light to all who grieve. Bathe their hearts in the grace and light of the resurrection. Holy God,
Hear our prayer.

God of the universe, your name is majestic in all the earth. We appeal to you to hear our prayers and the prayers of everyone in the world. We pray in the name of the Father, Son, and Holy Spirit.
Amen.

Sending Dialogue

We go with the love of God, our Father.
We will bring God's love to others.

We go with the grace of the Lord, Jesus Christ.
We will bring God's forgiveness and peace into the world.

We go in the fellowship of the Holy Spirit.
We will serve others where God calls us to serve.

Hymns

Come, Join The Dance Of Trinity
Come, Thou Almighty King
Eternal, Unchanging, We Sing To Thy Praise
Father Most Holy
God, Our Father, We Adore Thee
Holy God, We Praise Your Name
Holy, Holy, Holy, Lord God Almighty!
How Great Thou Art
I Believe In God Almighty
We Praise You, O God

Proper 3 / Ordinary Time 8

Isaiah 49:8-16a
Psalm 131
1 Corinthians 4:1-5
Matthew 6:24-34

Call to Worship
The heavens and earth sing for joy.
We all break forth in praise and exult our God.

God is here to comfort you.
We embrace the compassion of God.

You are inscribed on the palms of God's hands.
We are near to the mind and heart of God.

Collect / Prayer of the Day
Bring your love into the light, O God, and make us servants of Christ Jesus, and stewards of your mysteries. Clothe us with your love, deepen our faith, and strengthen us to live in the holiness of this day, with Christ our Lord. Amen.

Confession / Assurance of Forgiveness
The Lord will bring to light the things now hidden in darkness.
The Lord will disclose the purposes of every heart.

As servants of Christ and stewards of God's mysteries, we confess our sins.
{silent prayer for personal confession of sins}

Faithful God, we confess that we have not always been faithful servants, or trustworthy stewards of your word and your will. We have served other masters, sometimes letting worry dominate our lives, neglecting or taking for granted your provisions. Forgive us, O God, and draw us back to your heart. Remind us to daily place our trust in you, to serve you, and to place your reign uppermost in our words and actions. We pray in the name of Jesus, our Lord and Savior. Amen.

Servants of God, disciples of Jesus, God has heard your confession, both spoken and unspoken. His answer is clear: God is clothing you with divine, holy garments of peace, grace, and forgiveness. God forgives you for the sake of the one he sent to us, ✠ Jesus Christ, our Lord.
Amen.

Prayers of the People / Prayers of Intercession

Living God, strengthen and bless your church to be generous as an instrument of your compassion, that your hungry people will be fed, that the poor will be provided for, and that your glory will shine in the world you love. We turn to you Lord.
Lord, hear us as we pray.

Give us wisdom and holy reverence for the best use of the natural resources you have given us. Draw us away from abusing and destroying what you have given us.
Lord, hear us as we pray.

Strengthen and bless the nations with your wisdom and righteousness, that leaders would be moved to follow your ways of justice, care for the basic needs of all people, and put an end to greed, oppression, and violence. We turn to you Lord.
Lord, hear us as we pray.

Be present and lift up those who worry because they are unemployed, under-employed, or struggling to make ends meet. Send your Spirit, with divine inspiration and knowledge, to guide your servant church and all those who work for the betterment of society. We turn to you Lord.
Lord, hear us as we pray.

Give new life and compassion to those who are living without faith, or hope, or love. We turn to you Lord.
Lord, hear us as we pray.

We pray for all who suffer in mind or body, for all the sick, and for those who care for them. *(Specific names are included here).* We turn to you Lord.
Lord, hear us as we pray.

We pray for those who grieve. Turn their darkness into light. Send us to them to provide support and compassion. We turn to you Lord.
Lord, hear us as we pray.

We trust in your promises, O God, and we cling to our faith that you have promised to hear our every prayer. Answer us according to your holy will, in the Holy Spirit, through Jesus Christ, our Lord.
Amen.

Sending Dialogue

Go forth with a calmed, quieted soul.
We will serve only the Lord our God, as disciples of Jesus.

Go forth with a heart upheld and loved by God.
We will proclaim to the people that God, in Christ, will never forsake us.

Go forth, newly clothed with the glory of God's grace and love.
We will serve God's people, valuing each person as Christ has valued us.

Hymns

Be Still And Know
Count Your Blessings
For The Troubles And Suffering
He Leadeth Me
In God Alone
Jesus, Priceless Treasure
Seek Ye First The Kingdom Of God
Sent Forth By God's Blessing
What A Friend We Have In Jesus
You Satisfy The Hungry Heart

Proper 4 / Ordinary Time 9

Genesis 6:9-22; 7:24; 8:14-19
Psalm 46
Romans 1:16-17; 3:22b-28 [29-31]
Matthew 7:21-29

Call to Worship

God is in our midst.
The Lord our God is with us.

God is our refuge and our strength.
God is a very present help in trouble.

God is our stronghold.
We exalt God here, among the nations, and in all the earth.

Collect / Prayer of the Day

Teach us, O Lord God, teach us your ways. Build the foundation of our lives upon your love and your abiding presence. Place the gospel upon our hearts, and teach us to live by faith, through Jesus Christ, your Son, our Lord. Amen.

Confession / Assurance of Forgiveness

I am not ashamed of the gospel.
It is the power of God for salvation to everyone who has faith.

We confess our sins.
{silent prayer for personal confession of sins}

God of love, we confess that we have not always been wise in your sight. We have all sinned. We have heard your word, and foolishly ignored your word. We have failed to do your will in our daily living. We have broken your laws and commands. We have not treated our neighbors according to our commitment to live as disciples. We have not always been thankful for your generosity. Forgive us, O God, forgive us. Place your will and your grace in our hearts, that Jesus our Lord will be the foundation of our lives. In his name we pray. Amen.

Hear the good news: you are justified by God's grace as a gift, through the redemption that is in Christ Jesus. The glory of God is seen in his life, death, and resurrection. In ✠ Jesus Christ, God forgives your sins.
Amen. Thanks be to God. Amen.

Prayers of the People / Prayers of Intercession

God of new life, bless and equip your church to serve you in this time and place. Form us by your Spirit into compassionate, understanding, listening disciples. Prosper all we do to make your gospel known wherever we go. Incline your ear to us, O Lord,
Lord, hear us praying.

Anoint every nation with the desire and power to live together in harmony and understanding. Strengthen the leaders of the nations to open pathways to end disputes, not fighting each other, but fighting hunger, ignorance, disease, sin, and evil. Incline your ear to us, O Lord,
Lord, hear us praying.

Make your presence known in the troubled and the darkest places of the world, that your children would work together to end suffering, oppression, distress, homelessness, malnutrition, illness, and disease. Send forth your light and your healing. Incline your ear to us, O Lord,
Lord, hear us praying.

Give strength to those working for peace and justice. Sustain, encourage, inspire, and renew them in their work that all they do would be in accordance with your will. Incline your ear to us, O Lord,
Lord, hear us praying.

Send your loving care and compassion to those suffering the effects of intolerance, prejudice, and neglect. Strengthen the church and agencies that work to relieve the suffering. Incline your ear to us, O Lord,
Lord, hear us praying.

We pray for those who are sick. Send them your love in this time of need. *(Specific names are included here)*. Incline your ear to us, O Lord,
Lord, hear us praying.

Send your gift of grace to those grieving today over the loss of loved ones. Send the light of your resurrection into their hearts. Incline your ear to us, O Lord,
Lord, hear us praying.

Lord God, we bring these prayers to you, confident that your glory is saturating our lives, though Jesus Christ our Lord.
Amen.

Sending Dialogue

Go forth, having heard God's word, determined to live according to this word.
We will reflect the glory of God in our words and deeds.

Go forth with your life built upon the rock of your salvation.
We will reflect the glory of God in our words and deeds.

Go forth with the astonishing teachings of Jesus in your minds and hearts.
We will reflect the glory of God in our words and deeds.

Hymns

Built On A Rock
He Leadeth Me: Oh, Blessed Thought!
I Know Not Why God's Wondrous Grace
Jesus Calls Us; O'er The Tumult
Lord God Of Hosts, Whose Purpose Never Swerving
Lord Of All Hopefulness
My Hope Is Built On Nothing Less
O God, Our Help In Ages Past
Rock Of Ages, Cleft For Me
The Wise Man And The Foolish Man

Proper 5 / Ordinary Time 10

Genesis 12:1-9
Psalm 33:1-12
Romans 4:13-25
Matthew 9:9-13, 18-26

Call to Worship

Come before the Lord and praise God's name.
We rejoice in the Lord who loves us.

Come before the Lord to learn the will of God.
We rejoice in the Lord who has chosen us.

Come before the Lord and stand in awe of God.
We rejoice in the Lord who gives us life.

Collect / Prayer of the Day

God of love, speak to us and teach us your will. Enter into our every sickness and make us well. Come into our darkest, our lowest places, even the places of death, and give us life. Gather us together, bind us with your love, and set us on the path to follow Jesus our Lord, now and always. Amen.

Confession / Assurance of Forgiveness

Jesus proclaimed that he would heal the sick and call sinners to himself.
We come to Jesus for healing and forgiveness.

We turn to God for the healing and forgiveness we need.
{silent prayer for personal confession of sins}

God of mercy, we come to you with sickness of heart, mind, and soul. We confess that we have sometimes been lukewarm followers of Jesus in our daily living. We have not trusted your promises. We have received your love and care, but have, too often, kept it to ourselves. We have not been generous with our time, abilities, and forgiveness. We have rejected and turned away those you love. As Jesus received the sick, tax collectors, and sinners, we come with hope to receive his loving acceptance. We ask this in his name. Amen.

Fellow believers, God's mercy is upon us. The love of Christ Jesus, by his death on the cross, gives us new life, a fresh start. Receive now God's loving-kindness. Receive a renewed call to follow Jesus. Receive the forgiveness of your sins from God, through ✠ Jesus Christ, our healer and redeemer.
Amen.

Prayers of the People / Prayers of Intercession

God of our redemption, grant the church a renewed relationship with you, that all believers might experience your peace, your strength, your grace, and above all your abiding presence. Help us to be faithful followers of Jesus, as he travels with us on our daily journey. Open our minds, hearts, and hands to be ready to serve according to his call, for your glory. Merciful God,
Hear our prayer.

Let your love surround our country. Send your divine grace, wisdom, and guidance to our elected leaders, that they be devoted to the well-being of all people, and that, through you, our nation would be an inspiration to all nations. Merciful God,
Hear our prayer.

Grant wisdom and integrity to all the world's leaders, that they use their power and authority to bring health, safety, and hope to their citizens. Help them to close their hearts to every evil. Merciful God,
Hear our prayer.

Grant relief to those who are denied freedom in their religious beliefs, those who are suffering in prison, and those whose very lives are threatened because of their faith. Grant them protection, courage, and steadfast love. Merciful God,
Hear our prayer.

Awaken faith and grant your peace to all those who experience doubts, fears, and anxiety. Merciful God,
Hear our prayer.

Encourage those who suffer in body, mind, or spirit. Through Jesus, make them well. *(Specific names are included here).* Merciful God,
Hear our prayer.

Strengthen and sustain those who are in the depths of the sorrow of grieving. Grant them the comfort of the Holy Spirit. Surround them with the love and fellowship of a loving church family. Merciful God,
Hear our prayer.

Hear our prayers, O God, and answer us according to your will. In the name of Jesus we pray.
Amen.

Sending Dialogue

Go forth following Jesus, the great physician.
As Jesus heals us, we will bring healing to the world.

Go forth following Jesus, our divine teacher.
As Jesus teaches us, we will proclaim the loving-kindness of God.

Go forth following Jesus, merciful Savior.
As Jesus desires mercy, we will be merciful servants in his name.

Hymns

Healer Of Our Every Ill
How Deep The Father's Love For Us
I'm So Glad Jesus Lifted Me
Let Us Ever Walk With Jesus
O Christ, The Healer
O Jesus, I Have Promised
O Love Of God, How Strong And True
Through All The Changing Scenes Of Life
When Pain Of The World Surrounds Us

Proper 6 / Ordinary Time 11

Genesis 18:1-15 [21:1-7]
Psalm 116:1-2, 12-19
Romans 5:1-8
Matthew 9:35--10:8 [9-23]

Call to Worship
The kingdom of heaven has come near.
We call upon the name of the Lord.

The kingdom of heaven has come near.
We are servants of the Lord.

The kingdom of heaven has come near.
We gather in the Lord's house. Hallelujah!

Collect / Prayer of the Day
Almighty God, as your Son had compassion on the crowds, we rejoice today that he has compassion for us and for all people in the world. Fill our hearts today with his compassion and care. Empower and enlighten us to proclaim the good news and bring his healing and love into all the world. We ask this in the name of Jesus. Amen.

Confession / Assurance of Forgiveness
God's love has been poured into our hearts through the Holy Spirit.
While we were still weak Christ died for the ungodly.

We confess to God our weaknesses, and our ungodly thoughts, words, and actions.
{silent prayer for personal confession of sins}

O Lord God, we confess that we have been deaf to your voice. We confess that we have entertained unclean spirits. We have made ourselves to be lost, wandering sheep. We have not been compassionate. We have not labored for the kingdom. We have betrayed and injured our sisters and brothers. We have not let your peace rest upon the people in our lives. Forgive us, Lord. In your mercy and compassion, forgive us. Amen.

We have obtained access to God's redeeming grace. And so we boast in our hope of sharing the glory of God, for suffering produces endurance, and endurance produces character, and character produces hope, and hope does not disappoint us. God's love for us has proved that, while we were still sinners, Christ died for us. We are justified by faith, and we have peace with God, who forgives our sin, through ✠ Jesus Christ our Lord. **Amen.**

Prayers of the People / Prayers of Intercession

Lord of the harvest, we give you our greatest thanksgiving for all your children. As inheritors of the blessing of Abraham and Sarah, we thank you for your children throughout the ages, for prophets, teachers, leaders in the faith, including ordinary, faithful people. Increase our faith as we continue the journey given to us by Jesus. Saving God,
Hear our prayer.

We pray for all people in their daily life and work, that they may have joy in doing your will. We thank you for every blessing we have received from your bountiful hands. Direct your church to sow seeds of compassion among those who weep, seeds of joy among those who sorrow, and seeds of love in all the world. Saving God,
Hear our prayer.

Grant peace to all the nations of the world, especially those plagued by war, famine, disease, and threats of terrorism. We pray for all who govern, that they be open to your will. We pray for your wisdom and guidance upon those who work for justice. Protect the most vulnerable in the world, especially the children. Saving God,
Hear our prayer.

Send holy and divine patience, tolerance, kindness, love, and grace to every marketplace, business, school, home, and church. Let your love and grace abound in all places. Saving God,
Hear our prayer.

Protect and give grace to all in harm's way, men and women of the military, every family throughout the world touched by war and who fear for their lives, children who suffer, chaplains, doctors, nurses, and all caregivers. Let your healing power cure the sick, cleanse the lepers, cast out demons in all the world. Saving God,
Hear our prayer.

Strengthen and comfort the sick, the suffering, the sorrowful, the dying. *(Specific names are included here)*. Saving God,
Hear our prayer.

Comfort all who grieve, with the hope and peace of the resurrection. Saving God,
Hear our prayer.

Mighty God, give ear to our prayers, receive our thanksgiving, and send loving care to those we have named before you this day. We pray in the name of Jesus, Lord and Savior.
Amen.

Sending Dialogue

God calls us to bear witness to divine grace.
We will proclaim what God has done!

God calls us to bear witness to divine hope.
We will bring God's forgiveness and peace into the world.

God calls us to bear witness to divine love.
We will give and receive the compassion of Jesus!

Hymns

Alleluia, Alleluia, Give Thanks
For An Increase Of Laborers
Here I Am, Lord
I Love To Tell The Story
Lord Of All Hopefulness
Lord Of The Living Harvest
Lord, Take My Hand And Lead Me
Open Now Thy Gates Of Beauty
Sing To The Lord Of Harvest
Where Cross The Crowded Ways Of Life

Proper 7 / Ordinary Time 12

Genesis 21:8-21
Psalm 86:1-10, 16-17
Romans 6:1b-11
Matthew 10:24-39

Call to Worship
God will open our eyes and will be with us.
We worship the Lord and give glory to God's name.

Just as Christ was raised from the dead by the glory of the Father, we too will walk in newness of life.
We worship the Lord and give glory to God's name.

We will take up the cross and follow Jesus, and we will find life.
We worship the Lord and give glory to God's name.

Collect / Prayer of the Day
God of life and love, we acknowledge your Son, our Lord Jesus Christ. As he took up his cross for our eternal life, send us your Spirit that we would walk with him, even taking up the cross with him. Through his cross and resurrection, give life and love to us and to all the world. We pray in his name, Jesus our Lord. Amen.

Confession / Assurance of Forgiveness
Jesus died to sin, once for all. The life he lives, he lives to God.
We are to consider ourselves dead to sin and alive to God in Christ Jesus.

We approach God's throne of grace with repentant hearts.
{silent prayer for personal confession of sins}

Merciful and holy God, we confess that we have sinned against you, and against one another. We confess the sins that are a burden to us. We confess the sins that have burdened others. We have not given ourselves in love and service, as Christ gave himself for us. Forgive us, Lord, and give us life again. Amen.

The Lord is good and forgiving, full of mercy and compassion. God's steadfast love is certain. Brothers and sisters in Christ, as you turn to God with repentant hearts, know this: God forgives your sins, and gives you newness of life, through ✠ Jesus Christ our Lord.
Amen.

Prayers of the People / Prayers of Intercession

God of the sparrow, fill us with your own love, that we might value each creature and person of the human family as you do. Remind us daily that you are God of the rich and poor, the old and the young, the ordinary person, the children, the weak, the vulnerable. Help us to see your love in each person. Eternal God of love,
Hear our prayer.

Strengthen and increase the church in every land, and unite those who follow your Son, that the world would experience your love and be drawn to life in him. Eternal God of love,
Hear our prayer.

Let your presence be known within our nation, and in all the nations of the world. Touch the hearts of leaders, lawmakers, all public servants, and deliver them from oppressive actions, prejudicial behaviors, and every action that harms the well-being of your children. Eternal God of love,
Hear our prayer.

Give strength and inspiration to all who labor in the world in all types of professions, including doctors and nurses, teachers and

school staff, artists and musicians, laborers and office workers, firefighters and police officers, counselors, pastors, and therapists. Bless their work that it would be uplifting service to enhance the well-being of all people. Eternal God of love,
Hear our prayer.

Give your all-sufficient grace and hope to those with strong needs of body, mind, heart, and soul, including the lonely and afraid, the hungry and the homeless, the unemployed and the underemployed, the imprisoned and the enslaved, those with disabilities, the troubled, the addicted and their families, the seriously injured and the dying. Eternal God of love,
Hear our prayer.

Hear our prayers for the healing of the sick, the suffering, and those in pain. *(Specific names are included here)*. Eternal God of love,
Hear our prayer.

Grant your comfort and peace to all who are grieving, placing in their hearts your joyful promise of the resurrected life. Eternal God of love,
Hear our prayer.

Incline your ear, O Lord, and answer us. You abound in steadfast love to all who call on you. Preserve our lives and the lives of all your children, through Jesus Christ, our Lord and Savior.
Amen.

Sending Dialogue

Give thanks to the Lord, for God is good.
God's steadfast love endures forever.

God grant you courage, sending you forth to be disciples of Jesus.
We will take up our cross and follow him.

God's Holy Spirit be upon you to be faithful witnesses of Christ our Lord.
We will trust God and center our lives on Jesus.

Hymns

God Is Here
His Eye Is On The Sparrow
How Great Thou Art
Immortal, Invisible, God Only Wise
Lift High The Cross
Nearer, My God, To Thee
On Eagle's Wings
Take My Life, That I May Be
When Peace, Like A River
Will You Come And Follow Me? (The Summons)

Proper 8 / Ordinary Time 13

Genesis 22:1-14
Psalm 13
Romans 6:12-23
Matthew 10:40-42

Call to Worship
As we gather, we pray that God will give us divine light.
Look upon us and answer us, O Lord our God.

We pray that God will give us divine bountiful blessings.
Look upon us and answer us, O Lord our God.

We pray that God will give us divine, steadfast love.
Look upon us and answer us, O Lord our God.

Collect / Prayer of the Day
Holy God, holy and immortal, sanctify your people. Make us holy. Strengthen and inspire us this day that sin will not dominate our lives. Empower us to live in your grace. Grant us your free gift of eternal life, in Christ Jesus our Lord. Amen.

Confession / Assurance of Forgiveness
Do not let sin exercise dominion over you.
For sin will have no dominion over you, since you are not under the law, but under grace.

We confess our sins to our God, who invites each of us to experience new life in Christ.
{silent prayer for personal confession of sins}

Welcoming God, you offer us the treasures of your kingdom. You bless us with the gifts of your grace. And yet, we have refused these gifts. We have turned away from your reign through our sins of self-centeredness, stinginess, grudge-holding, disobedience to your will. Forgive us and restore us, O God. Call us away from everything which separates us from you, from each other, from your creation. Welcome us back to your divine heart. Deliver us from all our sins. Assure us again of your faithful love, through Jesus Christ our Lord. Amen.

In your repentance, God is freeing you from sin and creating a bond with you. The wages of sin is death, but know this: God is forgiving you, and giving you the free gift of eternal life, in ✠ Jesus Christ our Lord.
Amen.

Prayers of the People / Prayers of Intercession

Divine and Holy God, we thank you for calling us to be your people in the world. Strengthen and empower us to welcome all people, giving them cups of cold water, and all divine gifts you call us to share. We bring our prayer to you, O God.
Hear us, Loving God.

We ask you to send your light and your inspiration to our imperfect relationships with others. Unite us in your love, heal us, give us open minds to listen to one another, and a welcoming heart to serve. We bring our prayer to you, O God.
Hear us, Loving God.

Send your holy wisdom to all those in authority over the people of the nations of the world. Instill in them a desire to govern justly and honestly. Free those living in terror, oppression, and every kind of evil. We bring our prayer to you, O God.
Hear us, Loving God.

Grant that a spirit of hospitality be strong in our congregation and in the communities around us. Teach all your children to be kind, caring, and loving. We bring our prayer to you, O God.
Hear us, Loving God.

We give you thanks for all those who have encouraged us to have faith in you: parents and pastors, teachers, and friends. Give us the wisdom to gently bring others into your welcoming presence. We bring our prayer to you, O God.
Hear us, Loving God.

We pray for those who are sick, anxious, and suffering. Come into our presence with your all-sufficient love and grace as we pray for our needs. *(Specific names are included here)*. We bring our prayer to you, O God.
Hear us, Loving God.

We remember those you have welcomed into your eternal, heavenly home. Comfort us in our grief and bless the memories of our loved ones with your resurrection-love. We bring our prayer to you, O God.
Hear us, Loving God.

With bold confidence in your love, we place all for whom we pray into your enduring and ever-present compassion, through Christ our Lord.
Amen.

Sending Dialogue

God's will for us is that we live in a spirit of holy righteousness.
We go forth to live as instruments of holy righteousness according to the will of God.

God has made promises of hope and holiness to you.
We go forth, faithfully following the Lord Jesus as his disciples.

God creates a divine and holy bond to your hearts and souls.
We go forth daily keeping ourselves bound with God in faith.

Hymns

All Are Welcome
By Your Hand You Feed Your People
Have You Thanked The Lord?
In The Service Of The King
In The Singing
Lead Me, Guide Me
Lord Of Glory, You Have Bought Us
To Be Your Presence
When The Poor Ones
Ye Servants Of God

Proper 9 / Ordinary Time 14

Genesis 24:34-38, 42-49, 58-67
Psalm 45:10-17
Romans 7:15-25a
Matthew 11:16-19, 25-30

Call to Worship

Jesus said, "Come to me, all you that are weary..."
Loving God, embrace us with your gentleness and care.

Jesus said, "Come to me, all you who are carrying heavy burdens..."
Loving God, teach us your ways and place them on our hearts.

Jesus said, "I will give you rest."
Loving God, give peace to our hearts and rest for our souls.

Collect / Prayer of the Day

Father, Lord of heaven and earth, we seek to know you, and we desire that all people know you. Reveal yourself, your love, and your grace to us through your Son, Jesus Christ, our Lord. Amen.

Confession / Assurance of Forgiveness

Come to me, all you that are weary and are carrying heavy burdens, and I will give you rest.
Take my yoke upon you and learn from me.

For I am gentle and humble in heart, and you will find rest for your souls.
For my yoke is easy, and my burden is light.

We bring the light and the heavy burdens of our sin to God.
{silent prayer for personal confession of sins}

God of heaven and earth, through our Lord Jesus, you have promised you will give us rest as we carry our burdens, you will give us peace, and you will forgive us. We come to you confessing our sins. We confess those times we have become lost and separated from you, the times we neglected to bring peace to our relationships, when we spoke cruel words, when we created worthless divisions. We confess we have created burdens for others to carry because of our sins. We have often spoken of loving and doing your will, but we do not always do what we intend. Forgive us, Lord God, and restore us in our desire to delight in your law and your commands. Strengthen us to do those things that you love, in Jesus' name we pray. Amen.

The Lord our God is gracious and merciful, slow to anger, and abounding in steadfast love. God is good and compassionate to all of creation. God is faithful in every word, and gracious in every action. God upholds all who fall, and God raises up all who carry heavy burdens. Therefore, God forgives you all your sins, in the name of the Father, ✠ Son, and Holy Spirit.
Amen.

Prayers of the People / Prayers of Intercession

Holy God, we believe you desire the well-being of all your children. We give your thanks for every blessing of our lives, and we thank you for the countless blessings that are on the way in the days ahead. Open our eyes to see and appreciate your compassionate love for us. God of gentleness, rest, and love,
Hear our prayer.

Give grace to your church to be living witnesses and laborers, doing your work and will in the world, helping all those who are weary and carrying heavy burdens. Guide your church to places of need to bring rest, healing, and love to your children. God of gentleness, rest, and love,
Hear our prayer.

Send forth your Holy Spirit to government leaders, that they would diligently provide for the well-being of families, communities, countries, indeed the whole world. God of gentleness, rest, and love,
Hear our prayer.

Send your provision for the well-being of the earth. Bless all living things with life and growth. Protect and rescue all who struggle and suffer due to natural disasters. God of gentleness, rest, and love,
Hear our prayer.

Grant release and holy freedom to those who are perplexed and confused by rebellious forces within themselves. Send your healing to those who struggle with addiction, and every harmful behavior. Make your presence known to all those with these burdens. God of gentleness, rest, and love,
Hear our prayer.

We pray for the weary, the discouraged, the depressed. We pray for hope and healing for all who are sick, in pain, or in distress of any kind. *(Specific names are included here)*. God of gentleness, rest, and love,
Hear our prayer.

As we remember those who have entered into eternal rest and everlasting joy, grant peace to those who grieve the death of loved ones. Bless their memories and their tears of remembering. God of gentleness, rest, and love,
Hear our prayer.

Hear the prayers of your people, O God, and keep us always in your care. Give rest to all who are weary, bring relief to those with excessive burdens, and grant your love to everyone. In Jesus' name we pray.
Amen.

Sending Dialogue

God's name will be celebrated in all generations.
We will praise God forever and ever.

God will rescue us from sin, death, and evil.
We will speak God's truth and promises in our daily living.

God's wisdom will be revealed to you, in this generation.
We will live and love in ways that celebrate God's holy name.

Hymns

Christ The Worker
Day By Day Your Mercies Lord
Give Me Jesus
God Of Grace And God Of Glory
I Heard The Voice Of Jesus Say
Just A Closer Walk With Thee
Lead On, O King Eternal!
Praise To The Lord, The Almighty
Softly And Tenderly Jesus Is Calling
What A Friend We Have In Jesus

Proper 10 / Ordinary Time 15

Genesis 25:19-34
Psalm 119:105-112
Romans 8:1-11
Matthew 13:1-9, 18-23

Call to Worship

We gather to hear the word of God.
God's word is a lamp to our feet and a light to our path.

We gather to receive God's life.
Give us life, O Lord, according to your word.

We gather that God would make our hearts good soil.
Give us your spiritual food, O Lord, that the fruit of your Spirit would flourish among us.

Collect / Prayer of the Day

Almighty, life-giving God, plant the seeds of your word in the hearts of all your children. Enable every heart to become rich soil, receiving your word with understanding and joy. Grow your word so that, especially in times of trouble and persecution, your children would bear the fruit of your love, growing and producing your will in the world, through Jesus Christ our Lord. Amen.

Confession / Assurance of Forgiveness

Live according to the Spirit and set your minds on the things of the Spirit.
As followers of Jesus, the Spirit of God dwells within us.

With the Spirit of Christ within, we confess our sins.
{silent prayer for personal confession of sins}

O God of love, we come before you, wanting to purge all within us that impairs our relationship with you and with one another. We place before you all the wrong we have done, and your laws and commandments we have failed to keep. We have failed to let your word take root in our hearts, our faith has been shallow, our ears have not listened. We need your love, your grace, your forgiveness. Forgive us, renew us, and plant new seeds of grace and love in our hearts, through Jesus Christ our Lord. Amen.

Open your heart now to hear the good news: there is no condemnation for those who are in Christ Jesus. God, who raised Christ from the dead, gives life to your mortal bodies, and the Holy Spirit to your immortal soul. God forgives your sins, for the sake of ✠ Jesus Christ, our Savior and Lord.
Amen.

Prayers of the People / Prayers of Intercession

God of steadfast love, grant your saving power to the whole church on earth, providing good soil, yielding fruit, and proclaiming the good news of your mercy and justice. With open hearts and minds, we pray,
Hear our prayers, O Lord.

Rescue your creation from the bondage of sin, and all who neglect or even refuse to be good stewards of your call to care for the earth and the gifts you give us. With open hearts and minds, we pray,
Hear our prayers, O Lord.

We pray that the leaders of nations would become more and more committed to the well-being of your children. Draw them from the ways of oppression, injustice, greed, and division. Cast out any spirit of selfishness and bring them into your holy will. With open hearts and minds, we pray,
Hear our prayers, O Lord.

From the storehouses of the nations, send ministers and angels to provide food for the hungry, shelter for the homeless, protection for the exploited. With open hearts and minds, we pray,
Hear our prayers, O Lord.

Send forth your word, that your will may grow richly in the fields of our lives. Uproot the deep weeds and stubborn stones of sinfulness, in our families, places of work, schools and churches. With open hearts and minds, we pray,
Hear our prayers, O Lord.

Grant the healing power and grace of your presence to all who suffer in body, mind, or spirit. *(Specific names are included here).* With open hearts and minds, we pray,
Hear our prayers, O Lord.

Bring healing, comfort, and hope to all who are afflicted by grief. Lead them out of their darkness into the brightness of your saving resurrection-love. With open hearts and minds, we pray,
Hear our prayers, O Lord.

Gather our prayers unto yourself, O God. Hear us, answer us, and dwell within us. In the name of Jesus, we pray.
Amen.

Sending Dialogue

Set your mind and hearts on the things of God.
We will incline our hearts to God daily, to hear and witness to the good news.

Set your mind and hearts on teachings of Jesus.
We will incline our hearts to God daily, to live peaceably and lovingly with others.

Set your mind and hearts on God's Holy Spirit.
We will incline our hearts to God daily, in order to bear abundant spiritual fruit.

Hymns

Almighty God, Your Word Is Cast
As The Grains Of Wheat
For The Beauty Of The Earth
For The Fruit Of All Creation
Give To Me, Lord, A Thankful Heart
Lord, Let My Heart Be Good Soil
Lord, Speak To Us, That We May Speak
Lord, We Hear Your Word With Gladness
Open Your Ears, O Faithful People
Savior, Again To Your Dear Name

Proper 11 / Ordinary Time 16

Genesis 28:10-19a
Psalm 139:1-12, 23-24
Romans 8:12-25
Matthew 13:24-30, 36-43

Call to Worship

The Lord is in this place!
The Lord is with us now and always.

The Lord has called us together!
The Lord is blessing us in our gathering.

The Lord will teach us the ways of truth.
The Lord will keep us and will not let us go.

Collect / Prayer of the Day

Holy God, loving Father, your constant presence with us is life-giving. You know us as your beloved children. Joined by your Son, in the Spirit, you bless us with hope, and give us freedom from bondage. Plant the seeds of grace within us, make us holy in righteousness, and keep us as children of your kingdom, now and forever. Amen.

Confession / Assurance of Forgiveness

The Lord has searched me and knows me.
God is acquainted with all my ways.

We turn to God, confessing our sins, asking for forgiveness.
{silent prayer for personal confession of sins}

God of new life, we confess to you that we have not always let the fruit of repentance grow in our lives. We have done harm to our neighbor. We have wrongly judged. We have not walked in the truth. We have not forgiven, not served, not loved our neighbor as ourselves. Forgive us, gracious and loving God. Release us from bondage to sin and death. Renew us, strengthen us, and lead us in the way everlasting. In Jesus' name, we pray. Amen.

You are children of the kingdom of God, shining bright. You belong to Christ Jesus. You do not belong to the devil, the enemy. You belong to God, who removes your sins, casting them into the fire, forgiving you by the cross of ✠ Jesus Christ, our Lord. **Amen.**

Prayers of the People / Prayers of Intercession

God of mercy, we pray that your church will be a constant sign of hope and holy compassion in a world filled with weeds of sin, doubt, despair, and disobedience to your commandments and teachings. As we grow together in this often-hostile world, give your divine protection and growth to all who follow your Son and desire to live according to his teachings and example. Hear us, Lord.
You are merciful and loving.

We pray for the nations of the world, and for every leader and governing body, that they would adopt your vision of using their power and authority, resources and gifts, to care for the oppressed and the downtrodden. Keep them from abuse, exploitation, and injustice. Hear us, Lord.
You are merciful and loving.

We pray for those caught in hunger, poverty, addiction, and countless worldly struggles. Through your church, agencies of care, and generous people, provide for them their most basic needs. Hear us, Lord.
You are merciful and loving.

We pray to you for our families, and every relationship of our daily lives. Grant your divine love especially to families and friends in crisis, those who are struggling financially and with hardships, small and large. Grant them your wisdom, peace, and love. Hear us, Lord.
You are merciful and loving.

We pray for first responders, health-care workers, those in the military, and all who care for others in dangerous situations. Strengthen them, protect them, and guide them in all their endeavors. Hear us, Lord.
You are merciful and loving.

We pray for the sick and the suffering, that your healing graces be upon and within them. *(Specific names are included here)*. Hear us, Lord.
You are merciful and loving.

We give thanks for the example of those who died after living righteous lives and now shine like the sun in your kingdom. With this thanksgiving, we ask you to comfort those who mourn. Hear us, Lord.
You are merciful and loving.

Receive our prayers, Lord God, and answer them according to your holy and gracious will, for the sake of your Son, Jesus Christ our Lord.
Amen.

Sending Dialogue

Remember as you go: the Lord knows your heart.
We will sow good seeds of unity and peace in our daily lives.

Remember as you go: the Lord knows the paths you take.
We will sow good seeds of serving those in need in our daily lives.

Remember as you go: the Lord knows every word on your tongue.
We will sow good seeds of witnessing to the resurrection in our daily lives.

Hymns

God Is Here!
Guide Me Ever, Great Redeemer
Holy Spirit, Ever Dwelling
If You But Trust In God To Guide You
Jesus, Priceless Treasure
Jesus, The Very Thought Of You
Lord, Whose Love In Humble Service
Praise And Thanksgiving Be To God
Spread, Oh, Spread, Almighty Word
This Is My Father's World

Proper 12 / Ordinary Time 17

Genesis 29:15-28
Psalm 105:1-11, 45b or Psalm 128
Romans 8:26-39
Matthew 13:31-33, 44-52

Call to Worship

The kingdom of heaven is our refuge.
No burden will separate us from the love of God in Christ Jesus our Lord.

The kingdom of heaven is our treasure.
No power will separate us from the love of God in Christ Jesus our Lord.

The kingdom of heaven is our victory.
Nothing in all creation will separate us from the love of God in Christ Jesus our Lord.

Collect / Prayer of the Day

Living God, you have given us your Holy Spirit, who intercedes for us, strengthens us in every weakness, searches our hearts. In the Spirit, you are with us, loving us, always connecting and reconnecting us to your divine presence. In your deep love for us, we rejoice that you value and treasure us with all your heart. As we cling to Jesus our Savior, our treasure, we place our trust in you, Father, Son, Holy Spirit, now and always and forever. Amen.

Confession / Assurance of Forgiveness
What will separate us from the love of Christ?
Nothing in all creation will be able to separate us from the love of God in Christ Jesus our Lord.

Together we seek the forgiveness of our loving and gracious God.
{silent prayer for personal confession of sins}

God of mercy, we confess that we have connected ourselves too closely to material things and put our trust in them. We have not loved you with all our heart. We have not loved our neighbor as ourselves. We have sought worldly treasures and relied on them. We have failed to be examples of discipleship and commitment to the kingdom. Have mercy on us, O God, and forgive our sins. Plant the seeds of forgiveness in our hearts and let them grow and increase into the world around us. In Jesus' name we pray. Amen.

The God of love forgives you and frees you from your sins. God strengthens and heals you. God raises you to new life in ✠ Jesus Christ our Lord.
Amen.

Prayers of the People / Prayers of Intercession
Gracious Lord God, we pray for the church on earth in all its forms, that we may work together according to your will and the mission you have given to us. By your Spirit, guide us to plant seeds of the kingdom. Give us patience, and welcoming hearts, as you grow the seeds of your reign. We pray in confidence:
Hear us, God of love.

We pray for the well-being of our nation and all the nations of the world. Give elected and appointed leaders holy insight, wisdom, courage, and compassion that they work for justice, mercy, and peace in the world. We pray in confidence:
Hear us, God of love.

We pray for friends and neighbors, all who are experiencing difficult times. Send holy care and compassion to the unemployed and their families, the disabled, the grieving, all those who are lonely and isolated. We pray in confidence:
Hear us, God of love.

We pray that you equip loving, compassionate workers to the countless places around the world where there is disaster and suffering, injustice and false imprisonment, terrorism and torture, hatred and warfare, hunger and homelessness, disease and despair. We pray in confidence:
Hear us, God of love.

Send your kingdom — help all who suffer from depression or acute anxiety, the hungry, the homeless, the lost, those who can't break free from addiction. Give hope through the compassion of your church and agencies of caring. We pray in confidence:
Hear us, God of love.

Give the treasure of your healing to those who are sick, ill, and suffering. *(Specific names are included here)*. We pray in confidence:
Hear us, God of love.

As Christ Jesus died and was raised, and is now at your right hand, interceding for us, send to all who grieve the comfort, joy, assurance, and peace of the resurrection. We pray in confidence:
Hear us, God of love.

Hear our prayers, God our Father, blessing us and healing us according to your good will. In Jesus' name we pray.
Amen.

Sending Dialogue

God loved the world by giving us Jesus!
As the richness of God is within us, we will bring this divine richness into the world.

Our true and everlasting home is God's kingdom.
We will proclaim the good news that God will bring us into the joy of eternal life.

God will embrace us daily, and will work in and through us.
We will bring the kingdom of heaven to everyone around us.

Hymns

God, My Hope On You Is Founded
Guide Me Ever, Great Redeemer
Holy God, We Praise Your Name
Jesus, Priceless Treasure
Jesus, Thy Boundless Love To Me
Lord, Whose Love In Humble Service
Neither Death Nor Life
Seek Ye First The Kingdom Of God
Soul, Adorn Yourself With Gladness
The Kingdom Of God Is Justice And Joy

Proper 13 / Ordinary Time 18

Genesis 32:22-31
Psalm 17:1-7, 15
Romans 9:1-5
Matthew 14:13-21

Call to Worship
We gather here to speak the truth in Christ Jesus.
We come to praise Jesus, Messiah, Lord, and Savior, who is over all, and God-blessed forever.

We gather here for the nourishment Christ Jesus offers us.
Our hearts and souls are ready to receive what Jesus offers.

We gather here to call on the name of the Lord.
We come believing that the Lord is near to us.

Collect / Prayer of the Day
God of eternal generosity, you have always provided for your people, those who wandered in the desert, those who needed guidance and laws and promises, those who struggled to survive, those who were hungry. Your generosity is seen in Jesus, your Son, teaching and providing forgiveness, healing, compassion, and community. You have always given us enough, and more than enough. Fill us today with your compassion, patience, grace, forgiveness, and peacefulness. We thank you for the promise of eternal love, through the cross and resurrection of Jesus Christ our Lord. Amen.

Confession / Assurance of Forgiveness
The Lord is just in every way, and kind in every deed.
We praise the Lord and bless God's holy name forever.

We confess our sins, knowing that God is always willing to forgive.
{silent prayer for personal confession of sins}

Wondrous and generous God, we cannot earn your love and we do not deserve your generosity. You have already abundantly blessed us in your love. Yet we have turned away from you and lived in opposition to your will. We have failed in kindness, generosity, compassion, and forgiveness. Yet you do not deprive us of your love. Therefore, we humbly bow before you, asking for your forgiveness, though Jesus Christ our Lord. Amen.

You are God's child, blessed and made holy by God. Know this: God loves you and forgives you, by the cross of ✠ Jesus Christ our Lord.
Amen.

Prayers of the People / Prayers of Intercession

God, our great provider, grow within your church a spirit of generosity, so that, through the work of the church, the world would experience your generosity and loving care. Generous and loving God,
Hear our prayer.

We pray that leaders of the nations would incline their ears to you, and work to provide food, clean water, shelter, and safety for those entrusted to them. Generous and loving God,
Hear our prayer.

We pray for basic provisions for the poor and hungry, the widow and orphan, the homeless and the refugee. Provide them with meaningful lives, sending them ministers of hope. Generous and loving God,
Hear our prayer.

We pray for your missionaries throughout the world, for their strength and safety. We also pray for Christians who are persecuted around the world. Protect them, and grant them your steadfast love and mercy, as they bear witness to our Savior. Generous and loving God,
Hear our prayer.

We pray for this community of faith. Guide and inspire us to be generous in our giving and serving, that we share our abundance with those in need. Make us a living witness to your love. Generous and loving God,
Hear our prayer.

Grant nourishment, strength, and healing to everyone who struggles with any sort of adversity or sickness. *(Specific names are included here)*. Generous and loving God,
Hear our prayer.

We commend to your tender care all who mourn the loss of loved ones. Bestow within them your peace that passes all understanding, and the light of the resurrection. Generous and loving God,
Hear our prayer.

God, our Father, hear our prayers, and answer them according to your will, for the sake of your Son, Jesus Christ our Lord.
Amen.

Sending Dialogue

The crowds followed Jesus on foot from the towns.
We will follow Jesus wherever we go.

Jesus had compassion on the people and cured their sick.
We will share with others God's own compassion and healing power.

Jesus fed the crowds with overflowing abundance.
We will channel the overflowing abundance of God's grace, peace, and love, by the way we live.

Hymns

All Who Hunger
For The Bread Which You Have Broken
Let Us Break Bread Together
Love Divine, All Loves Excelling
O Christ, Your Heart, Compassionate
O Day Of Rest And Gladness
O Love That Will Not Let Me Go
Precious Lord, Take My Hand
The Church Of Christ In Every Age
You Satisfy The Hungry Heart

Proper 14 / Ordinary Time 19

Genesis 37:1-4, 12-28
Psalm 105:1-6, 16-22, 45b
Romans 10:5-15
Matthew 14:22-33

Call to Worship
We gather to worship our God, who speaks the words of peace we need in chaotic times.
We gather to follow Jesus, for he is here.

Glory to God, who leads us out of darkness and danger.
Glory to God who takes us by the hand and gives us hope.

The Lord is my strength and my salvation!
God's steadfast love endures forever!

Collect / Prayer of the Day
God of salvation, we come to you in faith, believing you are here, believing that you show up in the chaos and the storms of the world. We believe that you will never abandon us when we fail, when we sin, when we sink, when we create chaos. We trust that, when we cry out to you, you will catch us and hold us close to your heart, into your everlasting love. Reach out and save us, through your Son, our Lord and Savior Jesus Christ. Amen.

Confession / Assurance of Forgiveness
Glory be to God's holy name. Let the hearts of those who seek the Lord rejoice.
We will seek the Lord. We will seek God's strength. We will seek God's presence continually.

Remember the wonderful works God has done!
We give thanks to the Lord. We call on God's name. Lord, save us!

As disciples of Jesus Christ, we are called to struggle against everything that leads us away from the love of God and love of neighbor. I invite you now to confess your sins, asking God to lead you back into the love to which you are called.
{silent prayer for personal confession of sins}

God, our great redeemer, we confess that, in our struggle with the storms of life, we have failed to turn to you. We have failed to recognize your Son in the struggles of others. We have become self-centered and afraid. Forgive us these, and all our personal sins. Keep us in faith, open our hearts to trust in your love. Heal us, and forgive us our sins, that our hearts be at peace, that we might bring your peace into the world, through Jesus Christ, our Lord and Savior. Amen.

God has promised forgiveness of sins to those who repent and turn in faith. May God keep you in grace by the Holy Spirit, lead you to greater faith and trust, and bring you the peace of God's presence, through ✠ Jesus Christ our Lord.
Amen.

Prayers of the People / Prayers of Intercession

Loving and Almighty God, strengthen the church on earth to be a living sign of the presence of Jesus Christ in our world. Keep the church faithful to your will in every storm of our lives. God of peace,
Hear our prayer.

Inspire the leaders of every nation to diligently care for the weak, the exploited, the abused, the alienated, the forgotten, the misunderstood. We pray for peace in the world and an end to violence. God of peace,
Hear our prayer.

Restore and heal your creation, guiding us to be good stewards of all your gifts. God of peace,
Hear our prayer.

Protect those whose lives are threatened by dangers of nature, dangers of evil-doers, dangers of sin. Guide us to care for those in need. God of peace,
Hear our prayer.

Calm the storms and comfort all who grieve. Fill aching hearts with your peace and your hope. God of peace,
Hear our prayer.

As storms of illness abound, we pray for your tender care and your powerful healing to touch our friends and loved ones who are sick. *(Specific names are included here)*. God of peace,
Hear our prayer.

We give you thanks for the lives and witness of your faithful servants who now rest from their earthly labors. As we continue to navigate the stormy seas of life, with grief and suffering, we call upon you with confidence and hope. God of peace,
Hear our prayer.

Creator of the universe, calm every storm that disrupts our lives. Hear our prayers and rescue us, through Jesus Christ our Lord.
Amen.

Sending Dialogue

We go into a world where storms abound.
We will be ready for Jesus to reach out and save us.

We travel in a broken and dangerous world.
We believe that God, in Christ, will protect us.

We are sent into the world as God's people.
We will bring with us God's healing and peace.

Hymns

Eternal Father, Strong To Save
Great Is Thy Faithfulness
I'm So Glad Jesus Lifted Me
Just A Closer Walk With Thee
Lord Of All Hopefulness
My Hope Is Built On Nothing Less
My Life Flows On In Endless Song
Precious Lord, Take My Hand
We Have An Anchor
When Peace Like A River

Proper 15 / Ordinary Time 20

Genesis 45:1-15
Psalm 133
Romans 11:1-2a, 29-32
Matthew 15:[10-20] 21-28

Call to Worship
We gather to call upon the God of infinite love and mercy.
God's steadfast love endures forever!

We stand in God's presence, ready to receive God's word.
God's steadfast love endures forever!

We praise God who calls us here, that God will be glorified.
God's steadfast love endures forever!

Collect / Prayer of the Day
Loving and compassionate God, you love your children with unwavering, persistent love. You seek us to give us your eternal love, healing, and forgiveness. We cry out to you in our distress, in all our troubles. Save us, Lord. Lord, have mercy. Help us, Lord. We pray in the holy name of Jesus. Amen.

Confession / Assurance of Forgiveness
You were disobedient to God.
Lord, be merciful to us.

We confess our disobedience to God.
{silent prayer for personal confession of sins}

Merciful God, we confess that we have been disobedient to your word and your will. We have rebelled against you. We have not loved you with our hearts, souls, and minds. We have not loved our neighbors. We have judged ourselves and others as if that was our calling. Forgive our arrogance, O God. Teach us to listen more attentively to you. Forgive our disobedience. Forgive all our failures to love you, others, and ourselves. Have mercy on us, Lord, through Jesus Christ, our Lord. Amen.

Just as Jesus compassionately healed the sick, God is reaching out to you now in compassion to heal you of your sin. God forgives you through ✠ Jesus Christ, our Lord.
Amen. Praise God, the giver of mercy. Amen.

Prayers of the People / Prayers of Intercession

God of all creation, we give you thanks that your mercy extends to all people. Strengthen your church to show mercy in the world, through witness and acts of mercy in your name and for your glory. Lord, in your mercy,
Hear our prayer.

We pray that world leaders would work together for the wellness of all people. Touch the hearts of all who are in authority that they will embrace your desire for mercy, healing, and peace for all people. Lord, in your mercy,
Hear our prayer.

Send your calming Holy Spirit to bring peace where chaos and troubles reign. Bring healing to human relationship divisions and quarrels. Inspire your children to reconcile conflicts and reject oppression and terror of any kind. Lord, in your mercy,
Hear our prayer.

We pray for families burdened with troubles, trauma, hardship, estrangement. Send to their hearts your gifts of healing, forgiveness, and reconciliation. We pray that sin, self-centeredness, and stubbornness be uprooted from our relationships. Lord, in your mercy,
Hear our prayer.

We pray for those facing financial stress, the unemployed, stressed business owners and workers, the poor, the homeless. Send them the help they need, and your mercy through others, to protect them and enrich them according to your will. Lord, in your mercy,
Hear our prayer.

We pray for those whose illness, weakness, and suffering weigh them down. Hear them, Lord, as they cry out for mercy. *(Specific names are included here)*. Lord, in your mercy,
Hear our prayer.

Comfort those who grieve, especially those with depression, distress, hurt, and heartbreak. Wrap your loving arms around them. Bless their tears and bring healing to every broken heart. Lord, in your mercy,
Hear our prayer.

Generous God, we praise and thank you for your universal, unending mercy and loving-kindness. Hear the prayers we bring to you, through Jesus Christ our Lord.
Amen.

Sending Dialogue

God has filled our hearts with love and grace.
We will bring God's love and grace into the world.

As we go, we know we will sometimes tire from carrying heavy loads.
We will find rest and healing in Christ our Lord.

Proclaim to everyone what Jesus Christ has done for you.
We will proclaim and display the love and mercy of God!

Hymns

Fight The Good Fight
God Who Stretched The Spangled Heavens
How Great Thou Art
I Greet Thee, Who My Sure Redeemer Art
Just As I Am, Without One Plea
Let The Whole Creation Cry
My Faith Looks Up To Thee
Praise, My Soul, The God Of Heaven
Praise The One Who Breaks The Darkness
There's A Wideness In God's Mercy

Proper 16 / Ordinary Time 21

Exodus 1:8–2:10
Psalm 124
Romans 12:1-8
Matthew 16:13-20

Call to Worship
Blessed be the Lord, our protector and our strength.
Our help is in the name of the Lord, who made heaven and earth.

We give you thanks to you, O Lord, with our whole heart.
We sing your praise. We bow down and give thanks for your steadfast love and faithfulness.

We sing of the ways of the Lord, for great is the glory of God.
The steadfast love of God endures forever. Amen.

Collect / Prayer of the Day
Living God, you have called us into your kingdom, placing upon us the work of ministry. You have blessed us with the resources to bring your mission into the world. You have given us the keys to unlock your gifts of love, healing, forgiveness, service, compassion, caring for the hungry and the poor. Grant us your Holy Spirit and integrity to be your church in every place, through Jesus Christ our Lord. Amen.

Confession / Assurance of Forgiveness
Jesus is the Messiah, the Son of the living God.
Jesus is the Messiah, the Son of the living God.

We bow down before God confessing our sins, as disciples of Jesus.
{silent prayer for personal confession of sins}

Saving God, we have often proclaimed our faith in your Son, Jesus, our Lord and Redeemer. We have also denied our relationship with him. We have become conformed to the ways of the world, ways unacceptable to the ways of discipleship. We have been hard-hearted, sinful, and unfaithful. Forgive us, O God. Forgive us when we have lost our way and intentionally wandered off. By your Spirit, draw us back to your divine heart, through Jesus Christ our Savior and Lord. Amen.

God is gracious and merciful, abounding in steadfast love. This love is the good news of the gospel: "Christ Jesus came into the world to save sinners." God forgives your sins, in the name of the Father, ✠ Son, and Holy Spirit.
Amen.

Prayers of the People / Prayers of Intercession

Faithful God, as we proclaim this day that Jesus is Messiah, Lord, Savior, Redeemer, we come before you with thankful hearts, and a prayer that you strengthen, encourage us, and guide us to live our daily lives according to this faith. Incline your ear to us, O Lord,
Lord, hear us praying.

We pray for leaders in the church, that you would strengthen them in holiness and integrity of thoughts, words, and decisions. Protect your church from the temptations that can arise from leadership and authority. Teach your church true humility and foot-washing service. Build your church on the foundation of your love. Incline your ear to us, O Lord,
Lord, hear us praying.

We pray that your divine grace come down to every world leader and authority, that they would hear your will in their hearts. Conform their decisions and actions, not to the ways of evil, violence, and oppression, but to your perfect and holy will. Incline your ear to us, O Lord,
Lord, hear us praying.

We pray for the poor who live in neglected and unsafe communities around the world, those who are denied basic necessities of life, those living without adequate food or water, even a roof over their heads. Send ministers to give them hope and generous help. Incline your ear to us, O Lord,
Lord, hear us praying.

Heal divisions that fracture relationships, families, communities, and nations. Keep your children safe and help everyone, near and far, to live at peace with each other. Incline your ear to us, O Lord,
Lord, hear us praying.

We pray for those who are sick in body, mind, or spirit, and for those who care for them. Grant your healing, wisdom, and strength. *(Specific names are included here).* Incline your ear to us, O Lord,
Lord, hear us praying.

Send your comforting grace to those who grieve, lifting them and strengthening them by the power of your resurrection and the wonder of your presence. Incline your ear to us, O Lord,
Lord, hear us praying.

Holy God, we commit these prayers to you, trusting in your mercy, through Jesus Christ, our Lord and Savior.
Amen.

Sending Dialogue

Do not be conformed to this world but be transformed by the renewing of your minds.
We will seek to discern what is the will of God, what is good and acceptable and perfect.

Through God's grace do not think of yourself more highly than you ought to think.
We will live with sober judgment, according to the measure of faith that God has given us.

God has given you gifts according to divine grace and generosity.
As ministers of the gospel, we will be compassionate, loving, and generous according to God's grace.

Hymns

Before Jehovah's Awesome Throne
Built On A Rock
Christ Is Made The Sure Foundation
Here I Am, Lord
Lord, Speak To Us, That We May Speak
Love Divine, All Loves Excelling
Rock Of Ages, Cleft For Me
The Church's One Foundation
The Lord Jehovah Reigns
We All Are One In Mission

Proper 17 / Ordinary Time 22

Exodus 3:1-15
Psalm 105:1-6, 23-26, 45b
Romans 12:9-21
Matthew 16:21-28

Call to Worship
Salvation, glory, and power belong to our God.
We rejoice and give God all the glory.

We will glorify the holy name of God.
Our hearts will rejoice in the presence of the Lord.

We will sing songs of thanksgiving.
We will tell all the wondrous deeds of God.

Collect / Prayer of the Day
Mighty and eternal God, you have created your church to be building blocks of faith, with your Son, our Lord Jesus, as the cornerstone. He taught us the meaning and message of the Messiah, who would die for the salvation of the world. You have chosen us to deny ourselves, to take up our cross and follow him, to participate in bringing your children, and ourselves, back to you when we have lost our way. With the whole church, we embrace your gift of eternal life, through Jesus Christ, our Lord and Savior. Amen.

Confession / Assurance of Forgiveness
Seek the Lord. Seek God's strength. Seek God's presence continually.
We remember the wonderful works that God has done.

We confess our sins and commit ourselves to laying aside the works of darkness.
{silent prayer for personal confession of sins}

Eternal God of love, we confess that we have been mean-spirited. We have refused to adopt sacrificial love as our way of living. We have hurt others. We have adopted a selfish agenda, ignoring your holy agenda of love. We have not seen the seriousness of our personal sins, separating us from holy fellowship with each other, and doing harm to ourselves. Forgive us, Lord. Grant us your Spirit to help us push these sins behind us, out of our lives. Guide our lives, and prepare our hearts to receive your forgiveness. In Jesus' name we pray. Amen.

God, with divine mercy, strengthens you, gives you peace, and forgives you all your sins, through ✠ Jesus Christ, our Lord.
Amen.

Prayers of the People / Prayers of Intercession

Divine and Holy God, guide and inspire your church in the ways of genuine love, to minister according to what is good, and to love one another, and all people, according to your Holy Spirit. Compassionate God,
Hear our prayer.

We pray that you guide leaders of our nation, and the world, that they make decisions based on your divine love and mercy. We pray for an end of violence, bloodshed, and racism in our troubled world. Compassionate God,
Hear our prayer.

We pray for the lost and the confused, those who are seeking meaning in life. Help them find their way and enlighten them with clear signs of your reign and your presence in the world. Send us to be those signs and help us to live in your love. Compassionate God,
Hear our prayer.

We pray for those burdened by the cares of the world, those who worry, those plagued by anxiety, those distracted by temptations, those who are apathetic to goodness and truth, those who are hardhearted. Send them your grace, your gospel-teaching, and ministers of relief to care for their needs and their souls. Compassionate God,
Hear our prayer.

We pray for those who are troubled within themselves and in relationships. We pray for the hungry, the homeless, those living on the margins, refugees, victims of cruelty and evil. Help us to impart your blessings and goodness as the Body of Christ in the world. Compassionate God,
Hear our prayer.

Lay your healing hand upon those who are sick and suffering, those with demanding needs of body, mind, and spirit. *(Specific names are included here)*. Compassionate God,
Hear our prayer.

Send comfort, healing, and love to those who grieve the death of loved ones. Heal their pain, brokenness, and darkness of soul. Bless their tears, their laughter, all their memories. Give them hope and fill them with resurrection-life. Compassionate God,
Hear our prayer.

Faithful God, we lift our hearts and our voices to your eternal throne of grace. Through the Holy Spirit, we call upon your name. Hear our prayers and bless our lives, through Jesus Christ our Lord.
Amen.

Sending Dialogue

By his cross and resurrection, Jesus saved us and the whole world!
We will share God's love and the good news that Jesus is our Savior.

Our Savior Jesus Christ was lifted high on the cross for us.
We will remember and proclaim God's love for us in Christ Jesus.

Christ Jesus is the power and the wisdom of God.
We will take up our cross and follow Jesus, our Savior.

Hymns

Beneath The Cross Of Jesus
In Christ There Is No East Or West
Jesus, Still Lead On
Lift High The Cross
Lord Of All Hopefulness
Lord, Whose Love In Humble Service
O Master, Let Me Walk With You
O Praise The Gracious Power
Praise, My Soul, The King Of Heaven
Will You Come And Follow Me (The Summons)

Proper 18 / Ordinary Time 23

Exodus 12:1-14
Psalm 149
Romans 13:8-14
Matthew 18:15-20

Call to Worship
Praise the Lord! Sing to God a new song in the assembly of the faithful.
We praise God with our voices, with melody, and song.

All creation is praising the name of God.
The glory of the Lord overshadows heaven and earth.

Praise God, you people of God.
We praise God, whose name alone is exalted. Alleluia.

Collect / Prayer of the Day
God of heaven and earth, we experience your presence in worship, in the community of faith, in the forgiveness of sins, in prayer, in surprising and holy moments of love and grace, above all, in your Son. Send us your Holy Spirit, that gathered together, we would become more equipped to witness to the good news, so that the whole world would embrace your commandments, join together in fellowship, and receive your grace, through Jesus Christ our Lord. Amen.

Confession / Assurance of Forgiveness
Let us then lay aside the works of darkness.
Let us put on the armor of light.

Let us live honorably as in the day.
Let us put on the Lord Jesus Christ.

Let us confess our sins, asking God to help us cast off the ways of sin.
{silent prayer for personal confession of sins}

God of our salvation, we confess that we have not loved one another. We have not been obedient to the commandments you have given us. We have fallen asleep to your goodness and grace. We engaged in works of darkness. We have not lived honorably. We have quarreled. We have even glorified sin. Forgive us, O God, forgive us. Bring us again to your heart of love, into your divine light, and in true and holy fellowship with our sisters and brothers. In the holy name of Jesus, we pray. Amen.

Friends in Christ, salvation is near to us. God's love is here. God's armor of light is divine grace and is now surrounding your soul. Receive this word of good news: God forgives your sins, in the name of the Father, ✠ Son, and Holy Spirit.
Amen.

Prayers of the People / Prayers of Intercession

Ever-present God, you have called us to be the Body of Christ in the world, bringing light to darkness, reconciliation to brokenness, unity to conflict, love to hostility. Strengthen us in this vast ministry. Lord in your wisdom and mercy,
Hear our prayer.

Send your Holy Spirit to guide our government leaders in your ways. Guide them to do good in the world, to increase the well-being of the people, and establish peace and relief to war-torn and oppressed people. Inspire their hearts to put away every work of darkness. Lord in your wisdom and mercy,
Hear our prayer.

Restore your children, planting your peace and unfailing love in our families, friends, every relationship. Make forgiveness and reconciliation the desire of our hearts. Lord in your wisdom and mercy,
Hear our prayer.

We pray for all medical care workers and caregivers. Give them your strength, wisdom, and compassion. Lord in your wisdom and mercy,
Hear our prayer.

Grant your blessings and grace to teachers, students, and staff of our schools. Keep them safe every day, and inspire them to recognize your constant, abiding, holy presence. Lord in your wisdom and mercy,
Hear our prayer.

Grant restoration and healing to those who suffer from illness and anxiety. *(Specific names are included here)*. Lord in your wisdom and mercy,
Hear our prayer.

We give thanks for those who have gone before us to eternal glory. We remember their lives of service and their example of faith. In this remembering, comfort those who grieve. Lord in your wisdom and mercy,
Hear our prayer.

Hear the prayers of your people, O God. In your mercy, grant us all that we need, keep us in your care, and strengthen us, through your Son, Jesus Christ our Lord.
Amen.

Sending Dialogue

We are the church in a world where darkness and sin abound.
By the way we live, we will bring the light of Jesus into the world!

We are the church in a world where sickness and anxiety abound.
By the way we live, we will bring the healing of Jesus into the world!

We are the church in a world where fear and sadness abound.
By the way we live, we will bring the gospel of Jesus into the world!

Hymns

All Creatures Of Our God And King
Blessed Assurance
Blest Be The Tie That Binds
Children Of The Heavenly Father
Come, Thou Fount Of Every Blessing
Go, My Children, With My Blessing
How Firm A Foundation
Make Me A Channel Of Your Peace
O For A Thousand Tongues
What A Fellowship, What A Joy Divine

Proper 19 / Ordinary Time 24

Exodus 14:19-31
Psalm 114 or Exodus 15:1b-11, 20-21
Romans 14:1-12
Matthew 18:21-35

Call to Worship
The Lord is my strength and my song.
God has become my salvation.

I will praise God, who is majestic in holiness, awesome in splendor, doing wonders.
We sing to the Lord, who has triumphed gloriously.

Bless the Lord, O my soul.
All that is within me, bless God's holy name.

Collect / Prayer of the Day
God of mercy, as disciples of our Lord Jesus, we belong to you. Your presence in our lives is our nourishment, our strength, our source of love. Grant us the power of your Holy Spirit so that forgiveness, mercy, and reconciliation may abound in the world. By our words and our actions, help us to clearly show the world that Jesus Christ is Lord, and that we live our lives for him, now and forever. Amen.

Confession / Assurance of Forgiveness
"Lord, if another member of the church sins against me, how often should I forgive? As many as seven times?"
"Not seven times, but I tell you, seventy-seven times."

God will forgive you. I invite you to confess your sins.
{silent prayer for personal confession of sins}

Forgiving God, we confess that we have been revengeful, resentful, disobedient, sinful children. We have neglected and turned away from your divine love. We have not always honored you with our hearts or our actions. We have judged and scorned others harshly, even condemning them. In your compassion, forgive us and grant us the grace of true repentance, in Jesus' name. Amen.

God is merciful and gracious, abounding in steadfast love, with over-flowing blessings of forgiveness. God enables you to live in Christ with new hope and a renewed strength to love. This is good news for you: God forgives your sins through ✠ Jesus Christ, our Lord.
Amen.

Prayers of the People / Prayers of Intercession

God of our redemption, we come to you in gratitude for strengthening us, and for guiding us by your Holy Spirit, enabling us to live our lives in Christ. We are thankful for your forgiveness and grace when we fail, and for renewing us with a new beginning. Lord, hear our prayer.
Have mercy on us and answer us.

Bind your church together in the fellowship of prayer, uniting heaven and earth. Free us, and all your people, from the prisons of hatefulness, sin, and evil. Grant us your light in the darkness. Lord, hear our prayer.
Have mercy on us and answer us.

Bless elected leaders of our nation, and of all the world, to make decisions with justice, courage, and compassion. Keep them ever mindful of your will, seeking the welfare of all people, especially the weak and vulnerable. Lord, hear our prayer.
Have mercy on us and answer us.

Calm and transform human tendencies toward violence, oppression, and hatred. Give us direction and insight to remove bitterness, jealousy, and indifference from our lives. Guide us to serve the poor, the weak, the exhausted, the abandoned, the lost. Lord, hear our prayer.
Have mercy on us and answer us.

Send your grace and love for the healing of the earth. Send relief to those suffering from natural disasters and weather-related hardships. Provide strength for those who give their time and energy to help those in need. Protect those who risk their lives in the service of others. Lord, hear our prayer.
Have mercy on us and answer us.

Send your healing presence, with caring people, to the lonely, the afflicted, the anxious. Give peace to all who are troubled. *(Specific names are included here).* Lord, hear our prayer.
Have mercy on us and answer us.

Comfort all who grieve, be present with them, dry their tears, and place in their hearts the radiance of the resurrection. Lord, hear our prayer.
Have mercy on us and answer us.

Hear our prayers, merciful God and pour out your grace and love upon all our requests, spoken and unspoken. Answer us according to your gracious will, through Jesus Christ our Lord.
Amen.

Sending Dialogue

We travel in a world where wickedness and greed abound.
We will follow Christ, bringing his grace and love wherever we go.

We travel in a world where selfishness and hate abound.
We will follow Christ, bringing his compassion and kindness wherever we go.

We travel in a world where sickness and sin abound.
We will follow Christ, bringing his healing and forgiveness wherever we go.

Hymns

Come, Ye Faithful, Raise The Strain
Forgive Our Sins As We Forgive
God The Omnipotent!
How Can A Sinner Know
Lord, You Give The Great Commission
O Christ, Your Heart, Compassionate
O Savior, Precious Savior
Spread, Oh, Spread, Almighty Word
When Morning Gilds The Skies
When We Are Living

Proper 20 / Ordinary Time 25

Exodus 16:2-15
Psalm 105:1-6, 37-45
Philippians 1:21-30
Matthew 20:1-16

Call to Worship
We draw near to God with a true heart.
We praise and magnify the name of God!

Give thanks to the Lord and call on God's name.
We sing praises to God, proclaiming the wonderful works of the Lord.

Great is the Lord and greatly to be praised.
We praise God's name now and forever. Amen.

Collect / Prayer of the Day
Lord our God, you are generous, and your grace overflows in all the world. Your grace rains down upon everyone, the just and the unjust, the rich and the poor, the righteous and the unrighteous. You are generous beyond our understanding, in the fellowship of the church, in our daily lives, in the whole world. We give you thanks in the name of Jesus Christ, our Lord. Amen.

Confession / Assurance of Forgiveness
The Lord God loves all people and calls everyone to repentance.
God is a gracious God and merciful, slow to anger, abounding in steadfast love.

Ponder, now, your sins. Bring them to God in a spirit of repentance.
{silent prayer for personal confession of sins}

God of heaven, we confess our sins. We have turned from you, complaining against your will and guidance. We have not been fruitful laborers in your kingdom. We have not lived our lives in a manner worthy of the gospel. We have been slow to love, slow to compassion, slow to serve. Forgive us, renew us, and restore us to be faithful disciples and servants of your reign, through Christ our Lord. Amen.

God comes to us in his Son, offering us forgiveness and new life. God has heard your confession. Therefore, be assured and confident that God forgives your sins through the life, death, and resurrection of ✠ Jesus Christ, our Lord and Savior.
Amen.

Prayers of the People / Prayers of Intercession

God of creation, we pray for the church to always be open to your Spirit's guidance for growth, bringing your love to all the people of the world. Inspire the church to find new and fresh ways to proclaim the gospel. We turn to you Lord.
Lord, hear us as we pray.

Grant healing in our community, in our region, and across the earth where there has been destruction, disaster, or calamity. We turn to you Lord.
Lord, hear us as we pray.

We pray for reconciliation between nations and for peace on earth. Send your Holy Spirit to guide world leaders in the ways of peace and justice, according to your will. We turn to you Lord.
Lord, hear us as we pray.

Send your loving care and daily bread to those who are alone and abandoned, to those enveloped in dark clouds of depression, to those overburdened and needy in body, mind, or spirit. We turn to you Lord.
Lord, hear us as we pray.

We pray for those who struggle against injustice in violent and oppressive places. Raise up those who will channel your peace and healing. We turn to you Lord.
Lord, hear us as we pray.

We pray for the sick and the suffering, that your healing graces come upon them directly and through caregivers. Bring them to wellness, with peace and healing for their hearts, minds, and bodies. *(Specific names are included here)*. We turn to you Lord.
Lord, hear us as we pray.

Comfort those in sorrow and grief, that they may know your peace. We pray that they clearly hear your promise of eternal life. We turn to you Lord.
Lord, hear us as we pray.

We lift before you, O God, our prayers, trusting in your loving presence and grace. Hear us in the name of Jesus our Lord.
Amen.

Sending Dialogue

People of God, live your lives in a manner worthy of the gospel of Christ.
We will labor, standing firm, working side by side, with faith in the gospel.

Go forth, with growth in the Holy Spirit, and joy in faith.
We will labor and bear fruit of love, generosity, and peace.

Christ Jesus leads you to labor in God's vineyard of grace.
We will labor with kindness, forgiveness, and generosity.

Hymns

Amazing Grace
Give To Our God Immortal Praise!
God Of Our Life, All Glorious Lord
God Will Take Care Of You
I Love Your Kingdom, Lord
Seek Ye First The Kingdom Of God
There's A Wideness In God's Mercy
We All Are One In Mission
Whatever God Ordains Is Right
With Joy We Meditate The Grace

Proper 21 / Ordinary Time 26

Exodus 17:1-7
Psalm 78:1-4, 12-16
Philippians 2:1-13
Matthew 21:23-32

Call to Worship
To you, O Lord, we lift up our souls.
In you, O God, we place our trust.

Give ear, O my people, to my teaching.
Incline your ears to the words of my mouth.

Teach us to know your ways, O Lord.
Guide us in your truth, God of our salvation.

Collect / Prayer of the Day
Good and loving God, you call us to work in your vineyard, as your own children, as the people of God, as disciples of Jesus your Son. Teach us, by your Holy Spirit, to know your will, doing what is right, just, and holy in your vineyard. As your perfect, obedient Son said "yes" to death, even death on a cross, give us grace to follow him and work in your vineyard with an obedient, holy "yes." In Jesus' name, we pray. Amen.

Confession / Assurance of Forgiveness
Christ humbled himself and became obedient unto death, even death on a cross.
Therefore, God highly exalted him, giving him the name above every name: Jesus Christ is Lord.

We humbly confess our sins before God in the community of faith.
{silent prayer for personal confession of sins}

Holy and eternal God, we confess that we have fallen short of the ways of your reign. As the church, we have not had the unity you desire. We have not loved others as your Son sacrificially loved us. We have been selfish and conceited, not seeing others as you see them. We have looked after our own interests, ignoring the needs of others. Forgive us, O God, in the name of your Son who died to reconcile us to yourself. Lead us away from selfishness, sin, and destruction. Lead us into a holy life of faith, hope, and love, through Jesus Christ, our Lord. Amen.

When you turn back to God, you truly live anew. God casts away from you all the transgressions you have committed. God is giving you a new heart and a new spirit! Rejoice in the mercy and steadfast love of God, who forgives our sins, and gives us the victory over sin and death, through ✠ Jesus Christ our Lord. **Amen.**

Prayers of the People / Prayers of Intercession

God of new life, we pray for your Holy Spirit to strengthen and guide the mission of your church throughout the world. Teach us to love as you love. Teach us to serve without counting the cost. Grant us integrity of heart and soul, that you be glorified in all our words and actions. We pray in confidence:
Hear us, God of love.

Guide the leaders of our nation, and all nations, into the ways of peace and justice, righteousness and truth. Strengthen and protect advocates and peace-workers in every nation. We pray in confidence:
Hear us, God of love.

Send and strengthen ministers, caregivers, and servants to care for the hungry, the sick, the stressed, the prisoner. Give them assurance of your love and your never-ending presence. We pray in confidence:
Hear us, God of love.

Unite us in common willingness to tackle the problems of our society and our world. Grant us your grace to overcome evil and improve the relationships of all people. We pray in confidence:
Hear us, God of love.

Grant your presence to those who are lonely, the discouraged, and those who struggle with heavy burdens. Grant them your strength and power. We pray in confidence:
Hear us, God of love.

Open your healing hand of love to all who suffer in mind, body, and spirit. *(Specific names are included here)*. We pray in confidence:
Hear us, God of love.

Grant strength, peace, and your presence to the dying. Grant compassion and mercy to those who suffer the loss of loved ones. We pray in confidence:
Hear us, God of love.

We lift our prayers to you, loving God, in the name of Jesus Christ our Lord.
Amen.

Sending Dialogue

Tell the world what Jesus has done and is doing still.
We will speak, according to God's will.

Clothe yourselves with compassion, kindness, humility, gentleness, and patience.
We will live, according to God's will.

Let all that you do be done in love.
We will love, according to God's will.

Hymns

All Praise To Him Who Reigns Above
Father, We Praise You
I Greet Thee, Who My Sure Redeemer Art
Jesus, The Very Thought Of You
Lord Jesus Christ, We Humbly Pray
Lead On, O King Eternal
My Faith Looks Up To Thee
O Jesus, I Have Promised
Open My Eyes, That I May See
Shine, Jesus, Shine

Proper 22 / Ordinary Time 27

Exodus 20:1-4, 7-9, 12-20
Psalm 19
Philippians 3:4b-14
Matthew 21:33-46

Call to Worship

The heavens declare the glory of God.
Holy, holy, holy is the God of the universe.

The Lord our God has rescued us from bondage.
We will love the Lord our God above all.

The very stone that the builders rejected has become the cornerstone.
This is God's doing and it is marvelous in our eyes.

Collect / Prayer of the Day

Lord our God, you have so loved our world, you have so loved us all, that you sent your Son to us. Give us your grace that we might truly know him, the cornerstone of faith and life. Through the power of his cross and resurrection, empower us, by your Holy Spirit, to press on toward the goal, our heavenly calling, where we will live with you in eternity, forever and ever. Amen.

Confession / Assurance of Forgiveness

Let the words of my mouth and the meditation of my heart be acceptable to you, O Lord.
You, Lord, are my rock, my strength, my redeemer.

We confess our sins in the depths of our hearts.
{silent prayer for personal confession of sins}

Lord, our redeemer, you have made your Son the cornerstone of your kingdom. He is the cornerstone of our faith. We confess that we have sometimes reduced him to a mere decorative part of our lives. We have rejected his divine authority, his commands, his cross. In so doing, we have been selfish, uncaring, revengeful, judgmental, unforgiving in our relationships with others. We ask you to forgive us, Lord, restore us, and redeem us. In the name of Jesus we pray. Amen.

Hear now the good news: just as God delivered the people of Israel from bondage, God delivers us from the bondage to sin and death, in and through ✠ Jesus Christ, our Lord and Savior. **Amen.**

Prayers of the People / Prayers of Intercession

God, our Father, we pray for your church on earth that, as your children and as disciples of your Son, we be willing deny ourselves, take up our cross daily and follow him. Lord God of life,
Hear our prayer.

We pray for the world which you love and redeem. Guide the leaders of the nations to recognize that you are Lord of all. Inspire them to make decisions and govern according to your will. Lord God of life,
Hear our prayer.

Keep us ever close to your heart and strengthen us to resist all kinds of temptations. Grant us gentle hearts with a willingness to forgive others. Grant us humility, openness of soul, and willingness to receive your Holy Spirit, reminding us of our own need for repentance and forgiveness. Lord God of life,
Hear our prayer.

By your Spirit, energize us to serve the poor and needy, those who suffer injustices. Grant that we would serve as Jesus served. Lord God of life,
Hear our prayer.

We pray for those enslaved by habits and addictions, that you would lead them to freedom and well-being. We also pray for their families, for wisdom and strength. Keep your children safe and loved. Lord God of life,
Hear our prayer.

We pray for your healing graces upon the sick and the suffering. *(Specific names are included here).* Lord God of life,
Hear our prayer.

We pray for those with sensitive, grieving hearts, remembering those who have died. Flood their souls with resurrection-light and peace. Lord God of life,
Hear our prayer.

Gracious and loving God, we come before your throne of grace with these prayers, humbly asking you to answer us in the name of Jesus our Lord.
Amen.

Sending Dialogue

Let your words be acceptable to the Lord, our rock and our redeemer.
We go forth to bear witness to what we have seen and heard.

Let your deeds and actions give glory to God.
We go forth to take our place in the world as servants of God's kingdom.

Let your daily living be centered in Christ Jesus our Lord.
We go forth to live as citizens of heaven, holding true to what God has given us.

Hymns

Forward Through The Ages
God Loved The World Of Sinners Lost
God Loved The World So That He Gave
Lord Christ, When First You Came To Earth
Lord Of The Dance
O Sacred Head Now Wounded
O Savior, Precious Savior
Shall We Gather At The River
Thine The Amen, Thine The Praise
You Are Holy

Proper 23 / Ordinary Time 28

Exodus 32:1-14
Psalm 106:1-6, 19-23
Philippians 4:1-9
Matthew 22:1-14

Call to Worship
The reign of God is cause for joy and celebration.
We praise the Lord, now and always!

Everyone is invited into the reign of God.
We give thanks to the Lord!

We are called to the kingdom of heaven.
We proclaim the wonders of our God!

Collect / Prayer of the Day
Loving God, you invite us into the kingdom of heaven to feast with your Son, to be nourished daily with your love, grace, forgiveness, and healing. You call us to witness that, in your Son, we are reconciled to you. Inspire us to proclaim the good news that all who hear may turn to you, through Jesus Christ our Lord and Savior. Amen.

Confession / Assurance of Forgiveness
Let your gentleness be known to everyone.
The Lord is near to all who call upon the name of God.

Let us now confess our sins before God and one another.
{silent prayer for personal confession of sins}

God, our maker and our redeemer, even as we rejoice in your reign and your presence, we confess that we sometimes have only served ourselves. We have neglected to care for the needs of others. We have been disobedient to your will. Forgive us every sin that has separated us from you. Transform us to receive and reflect your holiness, your love, your forgiveness, for the sake of Jesus Christ, our Savior and Lord. Amen.

The mercy of the Lord is from everlasting to everlasting. Whoever comes seeking forgiveness will not be turned away. Know that God forgives you through ✠ Jesus Christ, our Lord.
Amen.

Prayers of the People / Prayers of Intercession

Most holy and merciful God, send your Holy Spirit to your church and unite us. Help us embrace life with gratitude and thanksgiving. Guide us in the ways of service and love, according to your will. Gracious Lord,
Hear our prayer.

Send your peace that surpasses understanding to war-torn places in the world, places full of strife and conflict. Raise up leaders who will seek the common good, more than personal fame and fortune. Gracious Lord,
Hear our prayer.

Renew your creation, land, air, and water. Fill our hearts with loving care and concern for your creation. Gracious Lord,
Hear our prayer.

We pray for missionaries and those on mission trips throughout the world. Raise up faithful, loving, and compassionate witnesses to the gospel. Keep them safe and strong. Gracious Lord,
Hear our prayer.

We pray for those who are walking through the valley of death's dark shadows, and those who are troubled by sorrow, anxiety, despair, or confusion. Give them your divine strength. Revive their souls and refresh their hearts and the hearts of all who care for them. Gracious Lord,
Hear our prayer.

We name before you those who are sick, asking for your healing power. *(Specific names are included here).* Gracious Lord,
Hear our prayer.

Grant peace and comfort to those who suffer the loss of loved ones. Fill us with the light of the resurrection. Gracious Lord,
Hear our prayer.

We come to you, Lord God, in thanksgiving, bringing these our prayers and supplications. Hear the prayers for the praying-church in all the world. Hear us and answer us according to your will, in Jesus' name.
Amen.

Sending Dialogue

Stand firm in the Lord and let your gentleness be known to everyone.
We will stand firm in the love that God has given us.

Keep on doing what is honorable, just, pure, pleasing, and commendable before God.
We will stand firm in the faith that God has given us.

May the peace of God, which surpasses all understanding, guard your hearts and minds in Christ Jesus.
We will stand firm in the peace that the Lord has given us.

Hymns

All Are Welcome
Break Now The Bread Of Life
Come, Sinners, To The Gospel Feast
Gather Us In
Jesus, Lover Of My Soul
Lord, Take My Hand And Lead Me
O Love That Will Not Let Me Go
The King Of Love My Shepherd Is
Through The Night Of Doubt And Sorrow
When We Are Living

Proper 24 / Ordinary Time 29

Exodus 33:12-23
Psalm 99
1 Thessalonians 1:1-10
Matthew 22:15-22

Call to Worship
Give glory to God and praise God's holy name.
We give glory to God, creator of heaven and earth.

Give glory to God and keep God's commands.
We give glory to God, for we are God's people.

Give glory to God and worship only the Lord our God.
We give glory to God, for the Lord our God is holy.

Collect / Prayer of the Day
Great and awesome God, you know us by name, we have found favor in your sight, and you promise to be with us always. Your goodness and your steadfast love are ever before us and within us. By the power of the Holy Spirit, make us imitators of our Lord Jesus, serving in his name, rendering unto you our lives. In the name of Jesus, we pray. Amen.

Confession / Assurance of Forgiveness
God, our God, is forgiving and merciful.
God is gracious, abounding in goodness and love.

We turn to God, confessing our sins.
{silent prayer for personal confession of sins}

Holy and eternal God, we confess that we cling to cherished idols. We follow ways that do not belong to your reign, trying to fill our souls with worldly possessions. We have lived with unrighteousness, greed, and hypocrisy. Forgive us, O God, and restore us to yourself. Strengthen and renew us in your love, through Christ our Lord. Amen.

God has heard our prayer, our confession, our commitment to live our lives in Christ. God, who raised Jesus from the dead, rescues us and forgives our sins, in the name of the Father, ✠ Son, and Holy Spirit.
Amen.

Prayers of the People / Prayers of Intercession

O Lord, faithful God, we pray for your Holy Spirit to come down to the church in our day, that we be living examples of your Son. Renew and deepen the life of the church as a bearer of your love in the world. Compassionate God,
Hear our prayer.

We pray for those who struggle with their faith, and for those who do not believe. Grant them all a special measure of your love and grace. Compassionate God,
Hear our prayer.

Inspire the leaders of all nations to rule with justice and mercy. Send your Spirit into every nation and pour out your peace upon nations at war or in crisis. Compassionate God,
Hear our prayer.

Send your Holy Spirit to inspire all your children to render unto one another the kindness, forgiveness, compassion, respect, and love that you first give us. Compassionate God,
Hear our prayer.

Soften the hardened hearts of evil-doers, protect and heal those who are afflicted by oppression, abuse, prejudice, persecution, and assaults of every kind. Compassionate God,
Hear our prayer.

Heal those who are sick and restore them to wellness. *(Specific names are included here)*. Compassionate God,
Hear our prayer.

Comfort those who are sorrowful and grieve the deaths of loved ones. Comfort them with signs of your presence. Dry their tears, warm their hearts, give light to the darkness of their souls. Compassionate God,
Hear our prayer.

Loving God, we lift our prayers to you, trusting in the name that is above every name, Jesus Christ, our Lord.
Amen.

Sending Dialogue

God calls us to imitate Christ Jesus, as sisters and brothers in faith, steadfast in hope.
We will render unto God our relationships.

God calls us to turn away from every idol, and to grow in kindness and generosity.
We will render unto God our service.

God calls us to serve as examples of discipleship, laboring in love.
We will render unto God our lives.

Hymns

All Creatures, Worship God Most High
All People That On Earth Do Dwell
Glories Of Your Name Are Spoken
God, My Hope On You Is Founded
How Can A Sinner Know
I Want To Walk As A Child Of The Light
Lord, Keep Us Steadfast In Your Word
Our Father, We Have Wandered
Son Of God, Eternal Savior
We Give Thee But Thine Own

Proper 25 / Ordinary Time 30

Deuteronomy 34:1-12
Psalm 90:1-6, 13-17
1 Thessalonians 2:1-8
Matthew 22:34-46

Call to Worship
We gather to worship God.
We will worship with all our heart and soul and mind.

We gather to commit ourselves again to the ministry to which we are called.
We will love our neighbor as ourselves.

The favor of the Lord our God is upon us,
God gives us steadfast love. We rejoice in God all our days.

Collect / Prayer of the Day
Creator God, you formed the world in your holy love. You called a people to yourself. In the fullness of time, you sent your Son to redeem and restore the world. He taught us, and showed us, to love you and our neighbors as ourselves. By your Holy Spirit, teach us to love as Jesus loved. In his name we pray. Amen.

Confession / Assurance of Forgiveness
Blessed are those who do not take the path that sinners tread.
Their delight is in the law of the Lord.

We confess our sins to God who created us.
{silent prayer for personal confession of sins}

Eternal God, your love is everlasting. You always keep your promises to us. You never desert us. Your love is constant and abiding. Your love never fails. We confess that we have neglected to love as we ought to love. We have not loved those close to us. We have overlooked the strangers in our midst. We have shamefully mistreated our brothers and sisters in the world. Forgive us, Lord of love, for these and all our sins, in the name of Jesus. Amen.

Jesus Christ is the supreme example of God's love. This is what love is: not what we give to God, but rather what God gives to us. Hear this good news: God is now giving us the forgiveness of our sins, through ✠ Jesus Christ, our Lord.
Amen.

Prayers of the People / Prayers of Intercession

Merciful Lord God, bless the church on earth with a compassionate heart, and the strength to remain totally committed to discipleship, witness, and the ministry of loving and serving others. God of love,
Hear our prayer.

We pray for government leaders in all the nations of the world. Grant them caring and compassionate hearts, wisdom to make decisions for the well-being of people, and the courage to act according to your loving and just will. God of love,
Hear our prayer.

We pray for the peace and the well-being of all people, for wholesome education all over the globe, for an end to poverty, injustice, greed, and heartlessness. We pray for the refugees, the wanderers, those who are lost in our world, those who are homeless. Keep us aware of our calling to minister to all of these. God of love,
Hear our prayer.

We pray for those who are lonely, those with mental illness, those who are helpless and vulnerable. Send them caring people and agencies to minister to them. God of love,
Hear our prayer.

We pray for those among us who are troubled and those who carry heavy burdens, for those who are lonely, those in distress. Grant them the healing of your presence. God of love,
Hear our prayer.

We pray for those who have sickness or pain. Send your healing grace upon them. *(Specific names are included here).* God of love,
Hear our prayer.

Comfort and console those who grieve. Let them hear again the promise of new life in Christ Jesus. Give them your divine assurance of the resurrection. God of love,
Hear our prayer.

Hear our prayers, caring God, trusting that you are always working for good in the world. In Jesus' name, we pray.
Amen.

Sending Dialogue

You are entrusted with the message of the gospel.
We will love and serve God with joy.

God is blessing you with courage to proclaim the gospel of God in word and deed.
We will love and serve our neighbor with joy.

Go forth putting your faith into action, not for praise from mortals, but for the glory of God.
We will love and serve as the Holy Spirit leads and guides us.

Hymns

Come, Christians, Join To Sing
God Is Love, His Mercy Brightens
Goodness Is Stronger Than Evil
Jesus, Still Lead On
Lord, Thee I Love With All My Heart
Not For Tongues Of Heaven's Angels
Praise To The Lord, The Almighty
Put Thou Thy Trust In God
Sing Praise To God, The Highest Good
Spirit Of God, Descend Upon My Heart

Proper 26 / Ordinary Time 31

Joshua 3:7-17
Psalm 107:1-7, 33-37
1 Thessalonians 2:9-13
Matthew 23:1-12

Call to Worship
Give thanks to the Lord, for God is good.
God's steadfast love endures forever.

Let all the redeemed sing their praise together.
God's steadfast love endures forever.

I will go to the altar of God, the source of my joy.
God's steadfast love endures forever.

Collect / Prayer of the Day
Holy God, you call your church to attentively hear your word, and be dedicated to service. Send your Holy Spirit to establish integrity, gentleness, and humility in the church. Through the mission of the church, inspire your children in the world that, by our words and deeds, all would recognize your presence and love, and give you glory, through Jesus Christ our Lord. Amen.

Confession / Assurance of Forgiveness
God is the center of our faith.
God's love is the source of our hope and joy.

We approach God openly and honestly, confessing our sin.
{silent prayer for personal confession of sins}

Merciful and loving God, we have heard your word and your teachings. We know your commandments and your desire that we follow your holy ways. We confess that we have not always lived according to your word. We have judged others, even as we ourselves have sinned. We have been prideful and self-righteous. We have followed the ways of sin. Forgive us, Lord, heal the sin-sickness within us. Restore and renew us to a right relationship with you. Amen.

People of God, fix your minds and hearts on Jesus, the perfector of our faith, who has promised to be with us always. Through his presence now, believe this: God forgives your sins, for the sake of the crucified and risen one, ✠ Jesus Christ our Lord. **Amen.**

Prayers of the People / Prayers of Intercession

Lord our God, guide your church by the Holy Spirit to not only teach and preach your holy, divine word, but to put your word into practice. Keep your church pure and blameless. Strengthen the witness of the church in the entire world. Loving God,
Hear us when we pray.

We pray for the many children around the world crying for food and drink, for those drastically needing someone to provide for their most basic needs. Send them ministers to care for them. Loving God,
Hear us when we pray.

We pray for the abused, those who are victims of greed, those afflicted with disasters, those devasted by wars. Protect and send them healing and recovery. Loving God,
Hear us when we pray.

We pray for the leaders of nations, for every government, and for civic organizations. Bless them with genuine desire to be instruments and signs of your justice, love, and peace. Loving God,
Hear us when we pray.

Bless those who work in the world for peace and justice. We pray for social workers and those who work with the addicted, those with mental illness, and all who are stressed with life's trials. Loving God,
Hear us when we pray.

Send healing and care to those sick and suffering with disease, pain, weakened bodies, minds, and spirits. *(Specific names are included here).* Loving God,
Hear us when we pray.

We thank you for the lives of the faithful believers who have gone before us, for the teaching and example they have given us. Comfort those who deeply grieve as we remember these saints. Loving God,
Hear us when we pray.

Loving God, we entrust our all prayers and petitions into your hands, for the sake of Jesus Christ our Lord.
Amen.

Sending Dialogue

Live your daily life worthy of God and the grace you have received.
We will proclaim what God has done!

Live your daily life with upright and blameless conduct.
We will live according to God's commands.

Live your daily life practicing the word of God you have heard this day.
We will be compassionate and loving.

Hymns

Canticle Of The Turning
Come Down, O Love Divine
Gather Us In
God, My Hope On God Is Founded
Let The Whole Creation Cry
Love Divine, All Loves Excelling
May The Mind Of Christ, My Savior
Oh, Praise The Gracious Power
There's A Spirit In The Air
When In Our Music God Is Glorified

Proper 27 / Ordinary Time 32

Joshua 24:1-3a, 14-25
Psalm 78:1-7
1 Thessalonians 4:13-18
Matthew 25:1-13

Call to Worship
Let all who seek the Lord rejoice and be glad in God's presence.
We gather to praise God.

Incline your ears to the teachings of our God.
We gather to listen to God.

God will deliver and help us.
We gather to give thanks to God.

Collect / Prayer of the Day
O Lord God, by the light of your Holy Spirit, keep us alert, awake, and prepared for your presence in our lives. Open our eyes to see daily signs of your grace. As we proclaim our faith today that Christ Jesus died and rose again, empower us to live our lives for him, and inspire us on our journey to daily walk with him. Help us to be loving and compassionate as we proclaim the good news of your kingdom, through Christ our Lord. Amen.

Confession / Assurance of Forgiveness
With hope in God's promises, we believe will be with the Lord forever.
Yes, we will be with the Lord forever, and we encourage one another with these words.

In the presence of God, we confess our sins, with hope and faith in God's forgiveness.
{silent prayer for personal confession of sins}

Forgiving God, as disciples of your Son, we confess our sins and shortcomings. Even with strong faith, preparing for eternal life with you, we have sometimes been careless in obeying your commandments, reluctant to take up our cross and follow Jesus, we have hurt and insulted others. Forgive us, Lord, and rescue us from the bondage of our sins. Restore and cleanse us, bring us again to the joy of salvation, through Jesus Christ our Lord. Amen.

People of God, hear the gospel of love: "There is no condemnation for those who are in Christ Jesus." With repentant hearts, believe that God forgives you, in the name of the Father, ✠ Son, and Holy Spirit.
Amen.

Prayers of the People / Prayers of Intercession

God, our redeemer, we pray for your church. Prepare the hearts of believers to live as faithful disciples, to proclaim the gospel, to speak the truth in love. God of life,
Hear our prayer.

We pray for the leaders of our nation and our local community. Inspire them to open their hearts to receive your wisdom, to govern and lead with an understanding of your will for the well-being of all people. Remove greed of all kinds and grant them a spirit of compassion for citizens. We pray for an increase of justice and peace for everyone. God of life,
Hear our prayer.

Grant courage to believers and workers in agencies to go out into the darkness of the world to care for the poor, the homeless, the needy, the downtrodden, the oppressed, the lost. God of life,
Hear our prayer.

We pray for the well-being of the earth you have given us. Renew within us a deep desire to care for your creation. God of life,
Hear our prayer.

Send us daily reminders of your presence in our lives. Open our hearts to see the signs you give us. Remind us to see the face of your Son in the faces of all our sisters and brothers. God of life,
Hear our prayer.

Grant healing to the sick, grant your blessings, wisdom, and strength to every caregiver. *(Specific names are included here)*. God of life,
Hear our prayer.

We pray for those who grieve. Dry their tears, restore their hope, and comfort them with the light and warmth of the resurrection. God of life,
Hear our prayer.

We completely trust, O God, that you are attentive to the cries of our hearts, the desires of our souls. We give you thanks for every blessing, every answer to prayer, every good gift. In Jesus' name we pray.
Amen.

Sending Dialogue

Be prepared for the presence of God in your daily living.
We will tell of the glorious deeds of the Lord, and the wonders that God has done.

Be alert to hear God's word and God's will for daily living.
We will set our hope in God and keep God's commandments.

Be ready, and do not forget the marvelous works of God.
We will serve the Lord and carry God's grace and forgiveness to others.

Hymns

Arise, My Soul, Arise
Come, Sinners, To The Gospel Feast
O God Beyond All Praising
O Happy Day When We Shall Stand
Rejoice, Rejoice, Believers
Softly And Tenderly Jesus Is Calling
Soon And Very Soon
Teach Me, My God And King
Wake, Awake, For Night Is Flying
We're Marching To Zion

Proper 28 / Ordinary Time 33

Judges 4:1-7
Psalm 123
1 Thessalonians 5:1-11
Matthew 25:14-30

Call to Worship
We lift up our eyes to you, O Lord, enthroned in the heavens.
We lift up our eyes to you, beyond our worldly cares and troubles.

We lift up our hearts to you, O Lord, enthroned in the heavens.
We lift up our hearts to you, beyond our self-centered desires.

We lift up our minds to you, O Lord, enthroned in the heavens.
We lift up our minds to you, beyond our stresses and worries.

Collect / Prayer of the Day
Living God, giver of abundant gifts and daily bread, you richly bless our lives. Send your Holy Spirit to connect us to your holy presence and to one another. Unite us as a community of love, that the gifts you give us would serve your mission to bring all people to your Son. Move us to be trustworthy children of light, serving others and proclaiming the hope of salvation, through Jesus Christ our Savior and Lord. Amen.

Confession / Assurance of Forgiveness
God has not destined us for wrath.
God has destined us for obtaining salvation through our Lord Jesus Christ, who died for us.

Therefore, we now confess our sins to God with honesty of heart.
{silent prayer for personal confession of sins}

Merciful God, we have been sinful and selfish, wicked and lazy, distracted and deceitful. We have not always lived according to our abilities. We follow our own desires, with pride, greed, and neglect. In our sinfulness, we have lived as children of darkness. Forgive us, O Lord our God. Remove all that is sinful within us and bless all that is good and healthy. Restore us to your joy and peace. Direct, guide, and strengthen us to reconcile with our sisters and brothers according to your good and gracious will. In Jesus' name. Amen.

Hear this good news: by grace you are saved, though a faith that is not your own making. Your salvation is a gift of God. Through this grace, God forgives your sins and gives you new life, in the name of the Father, ✠ Son, and Holy Spirit.
Amen.

Prayers of the People / Prayers of Intercession

Most holy and merciful God, bless and empower your church on earth. As you bestow abundance upon each person, form the people of the church into faithful, self-giving servants. Loving God,
Hear us when we pray.

We pray for the nations of the world, that there may be peace among the people of the earth. Send calm in places with animosity, conflicts, and bitterness among the people. Open the hearts of government leaders to bring healing, reconciliation, and justice in every land. Loving God,
Hear us when we pray.

We pray for those who are confronted with outright evil in the world. Protect them and send believing servants and angels to minister to them. Grant compassion and insight to those who care for them. Loving God,
Hear us when we pray.

Grant us courage, wisdom, and creativity to use the gifts you have given us to bless others, bringing joy and peace. Loving God,
Hear us when we pray.

Bless our families and all our relationships, that the gifts you give us would help us to encourage and build each other up. Keep us from self-centeredness and greed. Teach us your ways of multiplying your grace in the world. Loving God,
Hear us when we pray.

Be the source of healing for those who are sick and suffering. Channel your healing power into the work of doctors, nurses, medicines, and every instrument of healing. *(Specific names are included here)*. Loving God,
Hear us when we pray.

As you have welcomed our loved ones into their heavenly home, comfort all who grieve, blessing our memories and our thoughts about them. Loving God,
Hear us when we pray.

Hear our prayers, God of eternity, and make our world prepared and ready to welcome you whenever and however you arrive in our lives, now, always, and forever.
Amen.

Sending Dialogue

God sends us out to bear witness to divine hope.
We will live in the abiding presence of God.

We can do all things that are needed, through Christ who strengthens us.
We will love with all our heart, all our soul, all our strength.

Encourage one another and build up each other, as indeed you are doing.
Whether we are awake or asleep, we will live with Christ.

Hymns

A Charge To Keep I Have
How Clear Is Our Vocation, Lord
Joyous Light Of Heavenly Glory
Let Us Talents And Tongues Employ
Light Dawns On A Weary World
Lord Of Glory, You Have Bought Us
May The Grace Of Christ Our Savior
O God, Our Help In Ages Past
Son Of God, Eternal Savior
We Are An Offering

Reign of Christ / Christ the King

Ezekiel 34:11-16, 20-24
Psalm 100
Ephesians 1:15-23
Matthew 25:31-46

Call to Worship
Come, let us sing to the Lord! Worship the Lord with gladness.
We come into God's presence making a joyful noise.

Enter God's presence with thanksgiving and praise.
We give thanks to God and bless God's name.

The Lord is a great God, a great king above all gods.
We worship the Lord our God, for we are God's people.

Collect / Prayer of the Day
God of our Lord Jesus Christ, Father of glory, creator of the universe, we join our voices and our hearts with all who praise the name of Jesus, whom you raised from the dead, and is now seated at your right hand in the heavenly places. We join with all believers of every nation on earth, all creation, heavenly beings, and the great host of saints in heaven, bringing our praise and worship to Jesus Christ, our Savior, Lord, and King, now and forever. Amen.

Confession / Assurance of Forgiveness
As shepherds seek their flocks, God will seek out the scattered sheep.
God will rescue us from days of clouds and thick darkness.

We now confess our sins, the moments we have strayed from God.
{silent prayer for personal confession of sins}

Almighty and merciful God, we confess that we have strayed from you like lost sheep. In our wanderings, we have sinned against you. We have followed the desires of our own hearts, not your will and your commandments. We have not cared for the hungry, the thirsty, the homeless, the sick, the suffering. Forgive us, O Lord, and have mercy on us. Rescue us, bind us back to your heart, strengthen and nourish us with your love, your mercy, your forgiveness, through Jesus Christ, our Lord. Amen.

Having confessed your sins, hear the good news as spoken by Jesus: "Come, you that are blessed by my Father, inherit the kingdom prepared for you from the foundation of the world." Know that, as inheritors of God's reign, God forgives you your sins, through the cross and resurrection of ✠ Jesus Christ, our Lord and king.
Amen.

Prayers of the People / Prayers of Intercession

Most holy God, we ask you for the strength and wisdom we need to stay connected to your reign, resisting every temptation to stray from your ways. Grant us your grace that we daily fix our minds and hearts on Jesus Christ, our Lord and King. Hear us, Lord of glory.
Lord, hear our prayer.

We pray for relief for those who are hungry in body or spirit, those who thirst for water or for love, the physically or spiritually poor, and all who are physically, mentally, or spiritually lost. Motivate and empower your church to provide all these persons with relief, loving care, and grace. Hear us, Lord of glory.
Lord, hear our prayer.

Deliver us from every kind of evil, darkness, and wrongdoing. Deliver the nations of the world from war, violence, injustice, terrorism, and oppression. As the shepherd of the people of the earth, feed the leaders of the nations with justice, and nourish them with peace. Hear us, Lord of glory.
Lord, hear our prayer.

Save and protect those who are in danger of harm because of selfishness, loneliness, and rejection. Hear us, Lord of glory.
Lord, hear our prayer.

Shower your healing graces upon the earth and upon those suffering from natural disasters. We pray for the well-being of all creation. Hear us, Lord of glory.
Lord, hear our prayer.

Strengthen the weak and bring calm and peace to the troubled, the injured, and the sick. *(Specific names are included here)*. Hear us, Lord of glory.
Lord, hear our prayer.

Send your healing Spirit to all who grieve. As our divine King has welcomed our loved ones into the eternal kingdom, we thank you for each one who has touched our lives in loving ways. Hear us, Lord of glory.
Lord, hear our prayer.

Hear our prayers, loving God. In your compassion and loving-kindness, answer us, strengthen us, and guide us, for the sake of Jesus Christ our Lord.
Amen.

Sending Dialogue

God raised Christ Jesus from the dead, giving him the name above every name.
Jesus is Lord! We give the glory due his name!

God has made Christ Jesus King over all things.
Alleluia! Praise the everlasting King! Alleluia!

We rejoice in the reign of Christ, who has all authority, power, and dominion.
We will live as ministers, servants, and disciples of Christ our king.

Hymns

All Creatures Of Our God And King
All Hail The Power Of Jesus' Name
Christ Is The King!
Crown Him With Many Crowns
Jesus Shall Reign
Lord, Take My Hand And Lead Me
O Christ, What Can It Mean For Us
O Worship The King
Rejoice, For Christ Is King!
Ye Servants Of God

Reformation

Jeremiah 31:31-34
Psalm 46
Romans 3:19-28
John 8:31-36

Call to Worship

In Baptism, we have been clothed in the likeness of Christ.
We are given new life in Christ, our Lord.

We are one in Christ Jesus!
We are inheritors of God's promises.

God's grace and presence is always with us.
"Your word is a lamp to my feet and a light to my path."

Collect / Prayer of the Day

Mighty and eternal God, we place our trust in you to always provide your church with grace, for the sake of the world. We thank you for the mission you give the church, for ongoing renewal in Jesus Christ, and for the guidance of your Holy Spirit. Above all, we thank you for Jesus Christ, crucified and risen for the world. Keep the church ever faithful to you, doing your will, serving others, and being an instrument of your grace, forgiveness, and love. In the name of Jesus Christ, our Lord, we pray. Amen.

Confession / Assurance of Forgiveness

The Word became flesh to dwell among us.
The Word is full of grace and truth.

We bring to the Lord our sins, asking for God's mercy.
{silent prayer for personal confession of sins}

Most holy God, we confess that we have sinned by not obeying your word. We have fallen short of your glory, day after day. Forgive us and restore us, O God. Write your law and your love upon our hearts. Free us from false beliefs and lead us to your divine truth. Free us from captivity to things of the world and lead us into lives of love and service. Free us from bondage to sin and grant us forgiveness, renewal, and a commitment to living our days as disciples of Christ Jesus. In his name we pray. Amen.

In the name of Christ Jesus, and by the authority of his word, I declare that God forgives your sins, in the name of the Father, ✠ Son, and Holy Spirit.
Amen.

Prayers of the People / Prayers of Intercession

Holy God, send down your Holy Spirit upon the whole church on earth. Lead us, guide us, unite us, and renew the covenant you have made with your people. Write your law upon our hearts so that all we say and do proclaims the grace you have shown us. God of salvation,
Hear us as we pray.

We pray that you strengthen, bring growth and renewal to all our ministries of teaching and serving. Keep us steadfast in your word. Help us to teach, preach, serve, and witness according to your will. God of salvation,
Hear us as we pray.

We pray for peace among the nations, and for wars to cease in all the world. Teach the leaders of every nation your ways of justice, mercy, and walking humbly in your presence. God of salvation,
Hear us as we pray.

We pray for those who struggle with living in poverty, hunger, exploitation, those affected by natural disasters, and disease. Bring reform to the world to relieve your children. God of salvation,
Hear us as we pray.

We pray for the safety and health of everyone in our schools, at work, and in our homes. God of salvation,
Hear us as we pray.

We pray for your healing upon all those who are troubled with grief, anxiety, pain, suffering, and illness. *(Specific names are included here)*. Restore them to health, hope, and joy. God of salvation,
Hear us as we pray.

We give thanks for all reformers of the church in every age, including those who work for holy reform and renewal in our day. Let their faithful service remain for us a witness and inspiration. God of salvation,
Hear us as we pray.

Hear our prayers, most merciful God, and grant us grace to entrust our lives and our world to your constant and abiding love, through Christ our Lord.
Amen.

Sending Dialogue

Christ Jesus is our delight and our salvation!
We will follow Christ and stand in his love.

Christ Jesus is a fountain of holiness within us.
We will live and proclaim the love of God in Christ!

Christ Jesus is the center of our lives.
By the Spirit, our "YES" to God is in Jesus our Lord!

Hymns

A Mighty Fortress Is Our God
Amazing Grace
For By Grace You Have Been Saved
God, Who Stretched The Spangled Heavens
God's Word Is Our Great Heritage
Let Us Ever Walk With Jesus
My Faith Looks Up To Thee
O God, Our Help In Ages Past
The Church Of Christ, In Every Age
The Church's One Foundation

All Saints

Revelation 7:9-17
Psalm 34:1-10, 22
1 John 3:1-3
Matthew 5:1-12

Call to Worship
Gathered as God's people, we are joined with the saints of all the ages.
Thanks be to God, who has qualified us to share the inheritance of the saints.

Thanks be to God for all the saints who have gone before us, whose robes are washed in the blood of the Lamb.
We give praise and glory to the God of all creation, the God we have come to know in Jesus Christ.

We are today's saints, in the living body of Christ, the church.
We praise the name of the Lord! Alleluia! Amen!

Collect / Prayer of the Day
God of heaven and earth, you have made us your children, created in your image, holy and good. Gather together, into your heart, all believers of every age, on earth and in heaven, and clothe us in your love, forgiveness, and mercy. Keep us holy and motivate us daily to continue to walk in the ways of holiness. Call us into passionate love for you, and instill within us passion to serve others, through Jesus Christ, who lives and reigns forever with you and the Holy Spirit. Amen.

Confession / Assurance of Forgiveness

Beloved, we are God's children. Rejoice and be glad. Your reward is great in heaven.
We are God's children. All praise and thanks to God!

We confess our sins before God and one another.
{silent prayer for personal confession of sins}

Holy and loving God, we confess that we have failed to love our families, our neighbors, even our enemies. We have neglected the poor and the hungry. We have not listened to the call of Jesus and followed him. We have not been faithful witnesses to him whose name we claim. Forgive us, O God, and bless us. Restore us to a right relationship with you and with our all sisters and brothers, through Jesus Christ our Lord. Amen.

People of God, in your desire to be forgiven, know this: you can taste the very forgiveness of God, who delights in you and loves you. Salvation belongs to our God. It is my joy and honor to announce to you: God forgives your sins and gives you a purified heart, in the name of the Father, ✠ Son, and Holy Spirit.
Amen.

Prayers of the People / Prayers of Intercession

God of our fathers and mothers, ruler of heaven and earth, throughout the centuries we have had spiritual giants and ordinary people as faithful witnesses to your goodness and love. For this great cloud of witnesses, we give you thanks. Help us this day to be faithful to the gospel we have heard, the good news that we have embraced. Eternal God of love,
Hear our prayer.

We pray for leaders of the nations. Inform their minds with knowledge of your will, soften their hearts with compassionate love, strengthen their wills with your desire for justice and peace. Eternal God of love,
Hear our prayer.

We pray for your church on earth, that we may remain faithful to the gospel, always striving for unity. We pray for missionaries around the world, and for believers undergoing persecution. Keep them in your care and bless their work and their witness. Eternal God of love,
Hear our prayer.

We ask you for your grace as we seek to live our daily lives with integrity as disciples. Teach us your ways and, by your Spirit, guide our steps and every path we take. Give us kind and gentle hearts in our work, school, home, and play. Give us wisdom in difficult decisions and stressful situations. Enlighten, transform, and guide us in our daily walk with you. Eternal God of love,
Hear our prayer.

Open the minds and hearts of those who do not know you, that, in their spiritual hunger, thirst, and deep longing, they would be drawn to your love. Help us to be witnesses of your love, with gentle and kind words, with silent caring, and with holy actions. Eternal God of love,
Hear our prayer.

Make your healing power and presence known to those who are suffering, grieving, confused, doubting, or in despair. Send them your compassion, blessing all those you call to care for them. *(Specific names are included here)*. Eternal God of love,
Hear our prayer.

We give you thanks for those who, after fighting the good fight of faith, have joined you in your eternal presence. As grieving people, we remember with affection and give thanks for those most recently departed from us. *(Specific names of the those who have died in the last year are included here).* Eternal God of love,
Hear our prayer.

Glory, honor, praise and worship to you, O Lord our God, in the name of Jesus.
Amen.

Sending Dialogue
Blessed are you who walk the way of our Savior.
We will live our lives as God's own people.

Blessed are you who love and serve your neighbor, and the poor.
We will live our lives as God's own people.

Blessed are you who proclaim the love and mercy of God.
We will live our lives as God's own people.

Hymns
For All The Saints
For All Your Saints, O Lord
Holy God, We Praise Your Name
How Great Thou Art
In Heaven Above
O Christ, Our Light, O Radiance True
Shall We Gather At The River
We All Are One In Mission
When Pain Of The World Surrounds Us
Ye Watchers And Ye Holy Ones

Thanksgiving

Deuteronomy 8:7-18
Psalm 65
2 Corinthians 9:6-15
Luke 17:11-19

Call to Worship
We come before our God with gratitude in our hearts, and with praise on our lips.
We give you thanks, O God, and we call upon your name.

We give thanks to you, O Lord, for you are good.
Your mercy endures forever.

You have chosen us to be your people.
We come before you with thankfulness and praise.

Collect / Prayer of the Day
Holy and gracious God, we worship you with grateful hearts and joyful spirit. You fill us abundantly with good things of the earth, and with the good things of your heart — your love, grace, compassion, healing, and mercy. We plead for your generous gifts to be given and shared with those who have great needs, especially where there is brokenness and adversity. We pray in the name of the one who gave his life for us, Jesus Christ our Lord. Amen.

Confession / Assurance of Forgiveness
God so loved the world that he gave his only Son.
Whoever believes in him will not perish, but will have eternal life.

Believing in Jesus, Son of God, we confess our sins.
{silent prayer for personal confession of sins}

Gracious God, we confess our sins, our failure of appreciating the gift of your Son and his daily presence in our lives. We confess our over-attraction and attachment to worldly things. We confess taking for granted your gifts of good health, the bounty of the earth, and the relationships of our lives. We confess greed, lack of sharing, and wastefulness. Blot out these and all our sins, O God, through Jesus Christ our Lord. Amen.

God, who has entrusted us with the ministry of reconciliation, forgives our sins and makes us well, through the cross and resurrection of ✠ Jesus Christ our Lord.
Amen.

Prayers of the People / Prayers of Intercession

Almighty God, on this day of joy and gladness, we lift our minds and hearts to you in thanksgiving and praise for the bounty of your love, and for all the good gifts you bestow on our lives. Generous God,
We pray and give thanks.

We thank you for your church. Keep us on the pathway of holiness. Grant that all who worship would do so in harmony, in spirit, and in truth. Bless the messages, the music, the silence, the prayers, the fellowship. Generous God,
We pray and give thanks.

We thank you for the countless ways you fill the emptiness of our lives with love and forgiveness. Send us your Spirit to teach us again, helping us to recognize your every gift. Generous God,
We pray and give thanks.

We thank you for the variety of gifts and the richness of different cultures you have given around the world. Help us to respect each other, and especially calm the clamor and quarreling of the people of every nation. Grant harmony and well-being to all your children. Generous God,
We pray and give thanks.

We thank you for our families, friends, and meaningful relationships. Strengthen these, and grant healing to relationships that are strained, stressed, or unhealthy. Send your divine love and grace. Generous God,
We pray and give thanks.

We thank you for the gift of medicine and science. We pray for those in need of healing in these days. *(Specific names are included here)*. Generous God,
We pray and give thanks.

We thank you for those significant people in our lives, that we have loved, and who are now in your eternal heaven. We thank and praise you for the resurrection. Touch the hearts of all who grieve, in the remembering, the tears, the laughter, the never-ending love. Generous God,
We pray and give thanks.

Holy God, holy and immortal, we bring these prayers to your loving care. Let your grace, love, and healing abound, through Jesus Christ.
Amen.

Sending Dialogue

God blesses us with abundant and overflowing gifts of love.
We will make known God's wondrous deeds among the people!

Remember the Lord your God, and every divine benefit.
We will not forget God's goodness. We will keep the commandments and follow the teachings of Christ.

Thanks be to God, who gives us the victory through our Lord Jesus Christ!
We will live with thanksgiving in our hearts, sharing God's love with everyone we meet.

Hymns

Come, Ye Thankful People, Come
For The Fruit Of All Creation
God Of The Sparrow
Great Is Thy Faithfulness
Let All Things Now Living
Now Thank We All Our God
Praise And Thanksgiving
Sing To The Lord Of Harvest
We Plow The Fields And Scatter
We Praise You, O God

APPENDIX 1
Prayers For Special Occasions

Mother's Day

We thank you for the women who gave us life. We give you thanks for every joy and blessing of motherhood. We pray that you give mothers your strength and compassion, especially those who are struggling to raise children, for those who are worried, frustrated, weary, or in strained relationships. We pray for stepmothers and foster mothers, navigating the joys and pitfalls of family life. We pray for mothers who have adopted, and those waiting for adoption. We pray for mothers who are sick and for their caregivers, especially care-giving children. We give you thanks and pray for all women who teach, lead, love, care for, and guide the children of others. Remembering mothers who have died, we pray that their light and love continue to shine on in our hearts and in our memories. We pray for mothers who grieve the death of their children.

Father's Day

God our Father, we pray today for all who love and nurture children, especially fathers, stepfathers, foster fathers, and all who serve as father-figures. Guide them to be good and holy role models to children. Mold them into your fatherly likeness. Give them grace and patience, that all their words and actions be loving. We lift our prayers for all who grieve the death of their fathers, and for fathers who grieve the death of their children.

Memorial Day

We give you thanks for the men and women who have died while serving our nation. We pray that their sacrifices will continue to serve the cause of peace, freedom, and justice for your children in the whole world. Comfort those who grieve and grant them your peace.

July 4th

We pray for this United States of America as we celebrate the birth of our nation. Make this county to be an instrument of your love and peace, that we may be a blessing to the world, and that, together, our nation may give you praise and glory. Even where there is division and hostility with each other, keep us united, safe from violence, and from harming each other in any way. We give you thanks for those who have endured hardships, even giving their lives, for our freedom. Guide us, God of all nations, to do your will. Keep us holy and make us a people who repent of our sins, always returning to you.

Labor Day

We thank you, Lord, for the gift and opportunity of labor. We pray that our efforts always be pure of heart, for the good of others, and to the glory of your name. We pray for all who labor in the marketplace, in factories and offices, in every profession. We lift up to you all who seek employment and those who work to defend the rights and needs of laborers everywhere.

Veterans' Day

Receive our thanks for every veteran who has served our nation faithfully and loyally. We pray for your protection and healing power for our veterans who experienced the stress and trauma of war and military conflicts, and who carry physical and mental wounds from their days of service.

Anniversary Of A Congregation

O God, our help in ages past, our hope for years to come, as we celebrate the anniversary of this congregation, we thank you for all your past blessings. We praise you for your daily presence, and we look to you with hope and guidance for our future.

APPENDIX 2
Classic Prayers

Thomas Aquinas
Grant me, O Lord my God, a mind to know you, a heart to seek you, wisdom to find you, conduct pleasing to you, faithful perseverance in waiting for you, and a hope of finally embracing you. Amen.

Bernard Of Clairvaux
Lord God, come quickly and reign on your throne within me! For something rises and tries to take possession of your throne; pride, greed, uncleanness and laziness want to be my kings. And then evil-words, anger, hatred, and a whole band of evil join the war trying to rule me. I resist them, I cry out against them. I say, "I have no other king than Christ." Christ, king of peace, come and reign on the throne of my heart. I will have no other king but you! Amen.

Søren Kierkegaard
Father in heaven! You have loved us first, help us never to forget that you are love so that this sure conviction might triumph in our hearts over the seduction of the world, over the inquietude of the soul, over the anxiety for the future, over the fright of the past, over the distress of the moment. But grant also that this conviction might discipline our soul so that our heart might remain faithful and sincere in the love which we bear to all those whom you have commanded us to love as we love ourselves. Amen.

Martin Luther
Lord God, heavenly Father, we know that we are dear children of yours and that you are our beloved Father, not because we deserve it, nor ever could merit it, but because our dear Lord, your only begotten Son, Jesus Christ, wills to be our brother, and

of his own accord offers and makes this blessing known to us. Since we may consider ourselves his brothers and sisters and he regards us as such, you will permit us to become and remain your children forever. Amen.

Charles H. Spurgeon

O, dear Savior, be not impatient with us, but still school us at your feet, until at last we shall have learned some of the sublime lessons of self-sacrifice, of meekness, humility, fervor, boldness, and love which your life is fit to teach us. O Lord, we beg you, mold us into your own image. Let us live in you and live like you. Amen.

Brooke Foss Westcott

O Lord Jesus Christ, in whom all differences of class are done away, take from us all pride, envy and prejudice. Unite us one to another by a common zeal for your cause and enable us by your grace to offer to you the manifold fruits of our service. Amen.

Yellow Hawk, Sioux Chief

Oh, Great Spirit, whose voice I hear in the wind, whose breath gives life to all the world, hear me. I come before you, one of your children, small and weak. I seek your strength and wisdom. Let me walk in beauty, and make my eyes ever behold the red and purple sunset. Make my hands respect the things you have made and my ears sharp to hear your voice. Make me wise so that I may understand the things you have taught. Help me to remain calm and strong in the face of all that comes toward me. Let me learn the lessons you have hidden in every leaf and rock. Help me seek pure thoughts and act with the intention of helping others. Help me find compassion. I seek strength, not to be greater than others, but to fight my greatest enemy - myself. Make me always ready to come to you with clean hands and straight eyes. So, when life fades, as the fading sunset, my spirit may come to you without shame. Amen.

www.ingramcontent.com/pod-product-compliance
Lightning Source LLC
Chambersburg PA
CBHW020944230426
43666CB00005B/159